English Reading and Spelling For the Spanish Speaker

Book 3

For Ages 10 - Adult

Written by
Kathleen Fisher

Illustrated by
Paul Widosh

Fisher Hill   Huntington Beach   California

Published by FISHER HILL
5267 Warner Avenue, #166
Huntington Beach, CA 92649-4079

Made in the U.S.A.

Publisher's Cataloging in Publication

Fisher, Kathleen S., 1952-
    English reading and spelling for the Spanish speaker. Book 3 / by Kathleen Fisher. --1st ed.
        p. cm.
        Audience: Ages 10-adult.
        Includes bibliographical references and index.
        ISBN 1-878253-26-3

        1. English language--Textbooks for foreign speakers--Spanish. 2. English as a second language.

Table of Contents

Contenido

Introduction

The purpose of this book is to help Spanish speakers learn to read and spell English. Book 3 builds upon the speech sounds, vocabulary, spelling, and comprehension skills developed in Books 1 and 2. As in the previous books, Book 3 uses a systematic approach to teach the English speech sounds for reading and spelling. Book 3 continues to provide practice with phonemic awareness, which is the ability to identify individual sounds and their order within words. Learning the different speech sounds will help students read and spell English fluently. Eighty-five percent (85%) of words in English are phonetic. Book 3 includes practice with suffixes and syllables. This book continues to present many of the small commonly used words, called sight words, that are not phonetic.

This book is bilingual since the word list for each lesson is presented in English and Spanish. There are pictures to go with many of the words in the lists. Each lesson emphasizes one or two new speech sounds. The vowel sounds in English are different than those in Spanish, but many of the English consonant sounds are similar to those in Spanish. There are 26 letters in the English alphabet:

Upper Case
A B C D E F G H I J K L M N O P Q R S T U V W X Y Z

Lower Case
a b c d e f g h i j k l m n o p q r s t u v w x y z

The five vowel letters are a, e, i, o, u. All the other letters are consonants. Consonants have one sound, except for c and g, which have two sounds. Vowels can make several speech sounds. Sometimes the letter "y" is used as a vowel.

Words are made up of syllables (units of pronunciation). Some words have one syllable, others have two or more syllables. Every syllable must have a vowel. If a word has three syllables then it has three vowel sounds.

Each lesson's word list begins with words that contain the speech sound that is being emphasized in that lesson. The last word or words in the list are sight words or homophones.

Practicing English speech sounds, sight words, and their spellings will help the Spanish speaker learn English reading and spelling.

Introducción

La finalidad de este libro es ayudar a las personas de habla hispana a leer y escribir en inglés. El Libro 3 expande sobre los sonidos del lenguaje hablado, el vocabulario y la comprensión desarrollada en el Libros 1 y 2. Como en los libros anteriores, el Libro 3 usa un planteamiento sistemático para enseñar los sonidos del inglés hablado al leerlo y deletrearlo. El Libro 3 continúa proporcionando práctica en la conciencia fonética, la cual es la facultad de identificar sonidos individuales y el orden que ocupan dentro de las palabras. Aprender los distintos sonidos del habla ayudará al estudiante a conocer la ortografía y a leer el inglés con fluidez. El ochenta y cinco por ciento (85%) de las palabras en inglés son fonéticas. El Libro 3 contiene prácticas con sufijos y sílabas. Este libro continúa presentando muchas de las palabras pequeñas usadas comúnmente llamadas "palabras de lectura automática" que no son fonéticas.

Este libro es bilingüe porque en cada lección se presenta una lista de palabras en inglés y en español. Hay dibujos que acompañan a muchas de las palabras de las listas. La mayoría de las lecciones subraya uno o dos sonidos nuevos. Los sonidos de las vocales en inglés son diferentes a los de las vocales en español pero muchos de los sonidos de las consonantes en inglés son similares a los de las consonantes en español. Existen 26 letras en el alfabeto en inglés:

Mayúsculas
A B C D E F G H I J K L M N O P Q R S T U V W X Y Z

Minúsculas
a b c d e f g h i j k l m n o p q r s t u v w x y z

Las cinco letras vocales son a, e, i, o, u. Todas las demás letras son consonantes. Las consonantes tienen un sonido excepto la c y la g, éstas tienen dos sonidos. Las vocales pueden tener varios sonidos en el lenguaje hablado. En ocasiones la letra "y" se usa como vocal.

Las palabras se componen de sílabas (unidades de pronunciación). Algunas palabras son de una sílaba, otras tienen dos o más. Cada sílaba debe tener una vocal. Si una palabra tiene tres sílabas, entonces tendrá tres sonidos vocales.

Cada lista de palabras de las lecciones comienza con palabras que contienen el sonido hablado que se está explicando en la lección. La última palabra o palabras de la lista son del vocabulario visual u homófonos.

Practicar los sonidos hablados en inglés, el vocabulario visual y su ortografía le ayudará a la persona de habla hispana a aprender a leer y escribir correctamente el inglés.

Lesson 1 * Lección 1

Word List * La lista de las palabras

Se añade un sufijo al final de una raíz o palabra base. Por ejemplo, consideremos *calling*: <u>call</u> es la palabra base e <u>ing</u> es el sufijo.

Inglés	Español
1. calling	llamando
2. fishing	pescando
3. playing	jugando
4. picking	recogiendo
5. looking	buscando
6. resting	descansando
7. parking	estacionando
8. flying	volando
9. dressing	vistiendo
10. locking	cerrando
11. growling	rugiendo
12. raining	lloviendo
13. both	ambos
14. sure	seguro

fishing

resting

growling

raining

1

Sentences * Oraciones

Lea las oraciones. Después escriba el número de la oración debajo del dibujo correcto.

1. Tom is looking for his cat.

2. Sam is locking the gate.

3. Pat is calling her friend.

4. The boys are playing at the park.

5. The dog is growling at the mailman.

6. Pam and Al are picking plums at the farm.

7. Jim is resting in the backyard.

8. Mom is parking the car.

9. Dan and Ken are fishing at the pond.

10. She is flying in a small plane.

Dibujos

a. _____

b. _____

c. _____

d. _____

e. _____

f. _____

g. _____

h. _____

i. _____

j. _____

Spelling Dictation * Dictado

Pídale a alguien que le dicte las palabras de la página 6. Después de escribirlas, LÉALAS y revise la ortografía. Corrija las palabras que estén equivocadas.

Fill in the Blanks * Llene el Espacio

Llene cada espacio con una palabra de la lista de palabras. Use cada palabra solamente una vez. Algunas oraciones tienen dibujos al final para ayudarle.

1. Why are you _____ your friend so late?

2. The dogs are _____ in the shade.

3. Kim is _____ the van on the street.

4. The men are _____ from the dock.

5. The kids are _____ up their toys.

6. Meg is _____ all of the windows in their home.

7. _____ boys are fishing at the pond.

8. They are _____ for the lost sheep.

9. It was _____ when we went camping.

10. The kids are _____ with the toys.

11. She is _____ in the bathroom.

12. The small dog is _____ at the big yellow cat.

13. He is _____ he left his bike at the farm.

14. He is _____ to Mexico to visit his mom.

Suffixes * Sufijos

El sufijo _ing_ es un sufijo vocal porque comienza con una vocal. Cuando se añade un sufijo vocal a una palabra que se termina con una vocal, la vocal final en la palabra base se elimina antes de añadirse el sufijo vocal. Ejemplo: _make_ se convierte en _making_.

Añada el sufijo vocal _ing_ a los siguientes verbos. (Recuerde que un verbo es una palabra de acción.) Cuando se añade el sufijo _ing_ al final de un verbo, eso significa que la acción está sucediendo ahora.

Base Word	Base Word with Suffix	Base Word	Base Word with Suffix
hike	1. _____	kick	6. _____
march	2. _____	hide	7. _____
vote	3. _____	sweep	8. _____
drive	4. _____	trade	9. _____
bake	5. _____	look	10. _____

Use cada uno de los verbos anteriores para llenar los espacios en blanco. Use cada verbo una vez.

11. I am _____ for the tall man.

12. The men are _____ up the hill.

13. The boy is _____ a stone.

14. The cat is _____ in the tree.

15. We are _____ our red car for a white truck.

16. She is _____ the porch.

17. Mom is _____ the van to the store.

18. We are _____ to the park.

19. Mark is _____ for his wool jacket.

20. Dad is _____ cupcakes for lunch.

4

WordSearch * Busca Palabras

Encuentra las palabras de la Lección 1 en el busca palabras. Marca las respuestas. Las palabras pueden estar escritas en forma normal, al revés o diagonalmente.

			dressing
locking	both	sure	calling
playing	picking	looking	parking

l	g	p	i	c	k	i	n	g	b	j
o	e	n	k	b	j	m	x	o	l	f
c	g	r	i	c	q	f	t	g	o	o
k	n	b	u	l	t	h	n	d	o	p
i	i	j	p	s	w	i	i	m	k	g
n	n	z	z	f	s	o	x	q	i	n
g	i	x	l	s	x	v	r	d	n	i
p	a	j	e	x	x	s	r	g	g	h
b	r	r	p	l	a	y	i	n	g	s
x	d	y	g	n	i	k	r	a	p	i
c	a	l	l	i	n	g	b	n	w	f

Answer Key * Las Respuestas

Sentences * Oraciones (page 2)

a. 6
b. 9
c. 5
d. 8
e. 3

f. 2
g. 10
h. 4
i. 1
j. 7

Spelling Dictation * Dictado (page 2)

dime, which, cooking, hook, belt, how, drift, picking, your, plain, robe, show, rainbow, crown, cake; The clown was all in red. The dogs will howl at the moon.

Fill in the Blanks * Llene el Espacio (page 3)

1. calling
2. resting
3. parking
4. fishing
5. picking
6. locking
7. Both

8. looking
9. raining
10. playing
11. dressing
12. growling
13. sure
14. flying

Suffixes * Sufijos (page 4)

1.	hiking	11.	voting
2.	marching	12.	hiking
3.	voting	13.	kicking
4.	driving	14.	hiding
5.	baking	15.	trading
6.	kicking	16.	sweeping
7.	hiding	17.	driving
8.	sweeping	18.	marching
9.	trading	19.	looking
10.	looking	20.	baking

WordSearch * Busca Palabras (page 5)

l	g	p	i	c	k	i	n	g	b	j
o	e	n	k	b	j	m	x	o	l	f
c	g	r	i	c	q	f	t	g	o	o
k	n	b	u	l	t	h	n	d	o	p
i	i	j	p	s	w	i	i	m	k	g
n	n	z	z	f	s	o	x	q	i	n
g	i	x	l	s	x	v	r	d	n	i
p	a	j	e	x	x	s	r	g	g	h
b	r	r	p	l	a	y	i	n	g	s
x	d	y	g	n	i	k	r	a	p	i
c	a	l	l	i	n	g	b	n	w	f

6

Lesson 2 * Lección 2

Word List * La lista de las palabras

El sonido /er/, como en *her*, se encuentra en la mitad o al final de una palabra. A menudo, al final de una palabra el sonido /er/ es un sufijo.

Inglés	Español
1. her	su
2. greener	más verde
3. slower	más lento
4. painter	pintor
5. farmer	granjero
6. sharper	más afilado
7. sticker	calcomanía
8. farther	más lejos
9. thicker	más grueso
10. under	debajo de
11. flower	flor
12. corner	esquina
13. busy	ocupado
14. full	lleno

painter

farmer

sticker

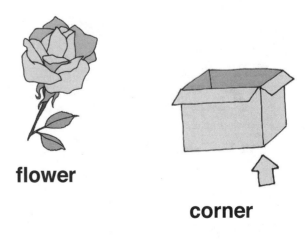

flower

corner

Sentences * Oraciones

Lea las oraciones. Después escriba el número de la oración debajo del dibujo correcto.

1. Your fishing rod is under the bed.

Dibujos

2. She has pink, red and yellow flowers in her yard.

3. The painter has a tall ladder.

4. Her home is on the corner.

a. _____   b.

5. The farmer plans to take his pigs to the market.

6. The small boy has a book full of stickers.

c. _____

7. Tom jumped farther than Dan.

8. The big truck goes slower up the steep hill.

d. _____

9. The grass is greener under the tree.

10. Dad is busy fixing dinner.

e. _____   f. _____

g. _____   h. _____   i. _____   j. _____

Spelling Dictation * Dictado

Pídale a alguien que le dicte las palabras de la página 12. Después de escribirlas, LÉALAS y revise la ortografía. Corrija las palabras que estén equivocadas.

Fill in the Blanks * Llene el Espacio

Llene cada espacio con una palabra de la lista de palabras. Use cada palabra solamente una vez. Algunas oraciones tienen dibujos al final para ayudarle.

1. The _____ milks his cows in the morning.

2. The vase is _____ of red and yellow flowers.

3. They are _____ painting their bathroom.

4. Your brown socks are _____ the chair.

5. She saw a pink _____ in her garden.

6. She plans to paint _____ bedroom white.

7. She will put a flower _____ in her book.

8. His home is _____ up the hill than mine.

9. He stood on the _____ waiting for the bus.

10. The fog is _____ today than yesterday.

11. Their grass is _____ than ours.

12. The _____ painted the walls brown.

13. He carved the stick to be _____ at this end.

14. The red snail is _____ than the green one.

Suffixes * Sufijos

Se añade un sufijo después de una raíz o una palabra base. El sufijo __ed__ es un sufijo vocal porque comienza con una vocal. Cuando un sufijo vocal se añade a la terminación de una palabra con una vocal, la vocal final de la palabra base se elimina antes de añadirse el sufijo vocal. Ejemplo: *bake* se convierte en *baked.*

Añada el sufijo vocal __ed__ a los siguientes verbos. (Recuerde que un verbo es una palabra de acción.) Cuando se añada __ed__ al final de un verbo, eso significa que la acción ya ha ocurrido. El sufijo __ed__ se pronuncia fonéticamente de tres maneras diferentes: /d/, /t/, y /ed/.

Base Word	Base Word with Suffix	Base Word	Base Word with Suffix
milk	1. _____	dine	6. _____
melt	2. _____	frown	7. _____
tape	3. _____	hike	8. _____
trade	4. _____	paint	9. _____
cook	5. _____	growl	10. _____

Use cada uno de los verbos anteriores para llenar los espacios en blanco. Use cada verbo una vez.

11. The ice _____ in the sun.

12. The man _____ at the small boy's trick.

13. Yesterday they _____ ten miles.

14. The painter _____ the walls green.

15. He _____ the show for his mom.

16. She _____ the cows in the morning.

17. Yesterday we _____ with our friends.

18. She _____ in her gray van for a red one.

19. She _____ a hot lunch for us.

20. The dog _____ at the small red fox.

WordSearch * Busca Palabras

Encuentra las palabras de la Lección 2 en el busca palabras. Marca las respuestas. Las palabras pueden estar escritas en forma normal, al revés o diagonalmente.

			her
under	thicker	greener	full
farther	sharper	busy	

j	y	f	r	e	n	r	o	c	s
s	r	s	a	q	z	i	c	c	t
r	e	c	u	r	e	o	n	v	i
e	k	e	d	b	t	g	l	v	c
t	c	h	a	j	r	h	c	b	k
n	i	u	n	e	u	f	e	p	e
i	h	e	e	n	u	z	r	r	r
a	t	n	d	l	s	n	p	e	r
p	e	e	l	k	y	q	y	w	h
r	r	p	r	e	p	r	a	h	s

Answer Key * Las Respuestas

Sentences * Oraciones (page 8)

a.	1	f.	6
b.	9	g.	3
c.	5	h.	4
d.	2	i.	10
e.	7	j.	8

Spelling Dictation * Dictado (page 8)

click, playing, sooner, book, milk, blow, camp, resting, were, rain, five, low, deeper, daytime, cow; The wool pants will soon fit you. Did you press the silk dress?

Fill in the Blanks * Llene el Espacio (page 9)

1.	farmer	8.	farther
2.	full	9.	corner
3.	busy	10.	thicker
4.	under	11.	greener
5.	flower	12.	painter
6.	her	13.	sharper
7.	sticker	14.	slower

Suffixes * Sufijos (page 10)

1.	milked	11.	voting
2.	melted	12.	hiking
3.	taped	13.	kicking
4.	traded	14.	hiding
5.	cooked	15.	trading
6.	dined	16.	sweeping
7.	frowned	17.	driving
8.	hiked	18.	marching
9.	painted	19.	looking
10.	growled	20.	baking

WordSearch * Busca Palabras (page 11)

Lesson 3 * Lección 3

Word List * La lista de las palabras

Las letras **–tch** producen el sonido /ch/, como en *match*. Regla: **-tch** se usa después de una vocal corta y generalmente al final de una palabra. De otro modo, el sonido /ch/ se escribe <u>ch</u> cuando sigue una consonante o un grupo de vocales, como en *ranch*, *speech*, y *porch*. Las últimas cuatro palabras en esta lista son excepciones de la regla.

Inglés	Español
1. match	fósforo
2. catch	agarrar
3. pitch	lanzar
4. switch	cambiar
5. patch	parche
6. witch	bruja
7. hitch	enganche
8. itch	comezón
9. hatch	salir del cascarón
10. crutch	muleta
11. rich	rico
12. much	cuánto
13. such	tal
14. which	cuál

match

patch

witch

hitch

hatch

crutch

13

Sentences * Oraciones

Lea las oraciones. Después escriba el número de la oración debajo del dibujo correcto.

1. The farmer has one crutch.

Dibujos

2. There is a brown patch on the knee of his pants.

3. We will hitch the trailer to the truck.

a. _____

4. The witch is riding a big broom.

5. How much milk do you want?

b. _____

6. He will strike a match to start the fire.

c. _____

7. The chicks will soon hatch out of the eggs.

8. The pitcher will pitch the ball to the catcher.

9. The rich man is stacking his dimes.

d. _____

10. Which dog belongs to Mark?

e. _____

f. _____

g. _____   h. _____   i. _____

j. _____

Spelling Dictation * Dictado

Pídale a alguien que le dicte las palabras de la página 18. Después de escribirlas, LÉALAS y revise la ortografía. Corrija las palabras que estén equivocadas.

Fill in the Blanks * Llene el Espacio

Llene cada espacio con una palabra de la lista de palabras. Use cada palabra solamente una vez. Algunas oraciones tienen dibujos al final para ayudarle.

1. Here is a _____ for the hole in your pants.

2. The _____ boy lives in town.

3. Which _____ owns the big black cat?

4. You have _____ a big foot.

5. Soon the snake will _____ from the egg.

6. The boy will _____ a fast ball.

7. May I _____ the red dress for the black one?

8. Strike a _____ to start the fire.

9. The bites on my arm _____ .

10. They will buy a _____ for their truck.

11. Who will _____ me when I jump?

12. Your _____ is under the desk.

13. How _____ rain did we get?

14. _____ farmer owns the brown cows?

Adding <u>es</u> * Adición de <u>es</u>

Añada <u>es</u> a las palabras que terminan en <u>s</u>, <u>x</u>, <u>z</u>, <u>ch</u>, o <u>sh</u>. De otro modo, añada una <u>s</u>.

Base Word	Base Word with Suffix	Base Word	Base Word with Suffix
match	1. _____	scratch	6. _____
painter	2. _____	hook	7. _____
buzz	3. _____	dress	8. _____
bench	4. _____	box	9. _____
kiss	5. _____	clown	10. _____

Use las palabras de la lista anterior para llenar los espacios en blanco. Use cada verbo una vez.

11. The _____ are fixing their small red car for the show.

12. The small witch _____ her big black cat.

13. The boy _____ the bite on his arm.

14. Hang the wet jackets on the _____ .

15. The brown _____ are stacked in the corner.

16. The big yellow bee _____ in the pink flower.

17. They are painting all of the _____ in the park.

18. The _____ are below the sink.

19. She has packed her two red _____ in the trunk.

20. The _____ are busy painting the big house on the corner.

WordSearch * Busca Palabras

Encuentra las palabras de la Lección 3 en el busca palabras. Marca las respuestas. Las palabras pueden estar escritas en forma normal, al revés o diagonalmente.

	catch	**pitch**	**switch**
rich	**much**	**such**	**itch**

h	i	a	j	h	c	t	a	h
n	c	t	s	h	c	t	a	p
x	h	i	c	w	w	v	c	v
h	c	t	r	h	i	r	q	t
c	t	o	a	c	u	t	h	t
t	i	d	a	t	m	c	c	n
i	p	t	c	u	u	h	f	h
h	c	h	c	s	v	v	d	u
h	z	h	m	a	t	c	h	x

Answer Key * Las Respuestas

Sentences * Oraciones (page 14)

a. 6
b. 3
c. 10
d. 2
e. 8

f. 4
g. 1
h. 9
i. 5
j. 7

Spelling Dictation * Dictado (page 14)

five, selling, brook, grain, itch, gone, town, harder, where, packing, cone, catch, growing, cupcake, darker; Tom ran slower than the rest of the boys. Are you telling me all of the facts?

Fill in the Blanks * Llene el Espacio (page 15)

1. patch
2. rich
3. witch
4. such
5. hatch
6. pitch
7. switch

8. match
9. itch
10. hitch
11. catch
12. crutch
13. much
14. Which

Adding es * Adición de es (page16)

1. matches	11. clowns
2. painters	12. kisses
3. buzzes	13. scratches
4. benches	14. hooks
5. kisses	15. boxes
6. scratches	16. buzzes
7. hooks	17. benches
8. dresses	18. matches
9. boxes	19. dresses
10. clowns	20. painters

WordSearch * Busca Palabras (page 17)

Lesson 4 * Lección 4

Word List * La lista de las palabras

Las letras –dge producen el sonido /j/, como en *badge*. Regla: Se usa -dge después de una vocal corta y generalmente al final de una palabra. De otro modo, el sonido /j/ se escribe -ge cuando sigue a una consonante, un par de vocales, o una vocal larga, como en *fringe, barge, page*.

Inglés	Español
1. badge	insignia
2. lodge	hotel/pabellón
3. edge	borde
4. fudge	caramelo
5. bridge	puente
6. judge	juez
7. pledge	promesa
8. ledge	cornisa
9. dodge	esquivar
10. budge	moverse
11. trudge	andar con dificultad
12. wedge	cuña
13. always	siempre
14. against	contra

badge

lodge

edge

fudge

bridge

judge

ledge

Sentences * Oraciones

Lea las oraciones. Después escriba el número de la oración debajo del dibujo correcto.

1. Do not let the glass fall off the edge.

2. The truck is parked on the bridge.

3. She will run and dodge the ball.

4. We will stay at the lodge in the forest.

5. Mom will put the fudge on the yellow plate.

6. Please cut a wedge of cheese for Pam.

7. They will trudge through the deep snow.

8. She has a badge on her jacket.

9. He always rests at noon.

10. Please put the fishing pole against the wall.

Dibujos

a. _____

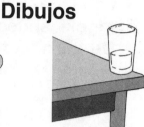

b. _____

c. _____

d. _____

e. _____

g. _____

h. _____

f. _____

i. _____

j. _____

Spelling Dictation * Dictado

Pídale a alguien que le dicte las palabras de la página 24. Después de escribirlas, LÉALAS y revise la ortografía. Corrija las palabras que estén equivocadas.

20

Fill in the Blanks * Llene el Espacio

Llene cada espacio con una palabra de la lista de palabras. Use cada palabra solamente una vez. Algunas oraciones tienen dibujos al final para ayudarle.

1. The _____ is busy all day.

2. Do not put the bikes _____ the car.

3. She wants only one _____ of cheese.

4. That plate is too close to the _____ .

5. They have boots to _____ through the mud.

6. The men stayed at a hunting _____ .

7. The big cat will not _____ from the mat.

8. There is a long _____ over the river.

9. The kids say the _____ in class every day.

10. Your flying _____ is in the box under the bed.

11. She will _____ the fast ball.

12. They sat on the _____ and ate a snack.

13. Sal is _____ on time.

14. Dad made _____ for everyone.

The Vowel e̱ * La Vocal e̱

La vocal e̱ es la letra de más uso en el idioma inglés. Algunas letras en el idioma inglés nunca se usan al final de una palabra, tales como j y v̱. Por lo tanto contamos con las terminaciones –dge y –ge por /j/, como en *lodge* y *page*. Las palabras que terminan con el sonido /v/ tienen el marcador mudo e̱ al final de la palabra. Use las siguientes palabras en las oraciones a continuación.

give	gave	live	live
bridge	have	hedge	smudge

1. We _____ on a busy street.

2. The cars and trucks are parked on the _____ .

3. The man _____ the tools to the farmer.

4. There is a _____ between the two yards.

5. I _____ fresh fudge for you.

6. Please _____ flowers to Meg who is sick in bed.

7. She ate a _____ bug.

8. The small boy has a dark _____ on his face.

El marcador mudo e̱ también evita que algunas palabras parezcan plurales. Use las siguientes palabras en las oraciones a continuación.

please	horse	house	cheese

9. Sam had _____ and eggs for lunch.

10. The _____ is resting in the barn.

11. _____ patch the hole in the wall.

12. It is raining at our _____ .

WordSearch * Busca Palabras

Encuentra las palabras de la Lección 4 en el busca palabras. Marca las respuestas. Las palabras pueden estar escritas en forma normal, al revés o diagonalmente.

			pledge
dodge	**budge**	**trudge**	**always**
against			

b	r	i	d	g	e	u	h	j	e
p	l	e	d	g	e	j	l	g	c
v	e	x	s	k	f	a	d	e	q
e	g	j	s	y	g	e	l	g	u
g	d	x	r	a	a	a	s	d	e
d	e	i	i	b	e	w	p	o	g
u	l	n	a	c	e	g	l	l	d
j	s	d	u	o	o	h	d	a	o
t	g	f	u	d	g	e	v	u	d
e	w	j	e	g	d	u	r	t	b

Answer Key * Las Respuestas

Sentences * Oraciones (page 20)

a. 3
b. 1
c. 2
d. 6
e. 5

f. 4
g. 8
h. 7
i. 9
j. 10

Spelling Dictation * Dictado (page 20)

stump, pile, painting, hook, drain, hatch, put, brown, corner, lodge, cracking, save, pitch, snowing, lipstick; The farmer is planting his crops. It was snowing all day long.

Fill in the Blanks * Llene el Espacio (page 21)

1. judge
2. against
3. wedge
4. edge
5. trudge
6. lodge
7. budge

8. bridge
9. pledge
10. badge
11. dodge
12. ledge
13. always
14. fudge

The Vowel e * La Vocal e (page 22)

1.	live	7.	live
2.	bridge	8.	smudge
3.	gave	9.	cheese
4.	hedge	10.	horse
5.	have	11.	Please
6.	give	12.	house

WordSearch * Busca Palabras (page 23)

Lesson 5 * Lección 5

Word List * La lista de las palabras

Las letras <u>aw</u> suenan /aw/, como en *jaw*. Regla: <u>aw</u> está por lo general al final de una palabra o seguida de <u>n</u> o <u>l</u>.

Inglés	Español
1. jaw	mandíbula
2. saw	verbo pasado de ver
3. paw	garra
4. lawn	césped
5. draw	dibujar
6. claw	garra/pinza
7. flaw	falla
8. pawn	empeñar algo
9. hawk	halcón
10. fawn	cervato
11. dawn	amanecer
12. crawl	arrastrarse
13. thaw	descongelarse
14. full	lleno
15. sure	seguro

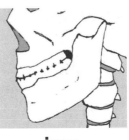

jaw

paw

claw

hawk

fawn

dawn

Sentences * Oraciones

Lea las oraciones. Después escriba el número de la oración debajo del dibujo correcto.

1. There is a thorn in the dog's paw.

2. The glass is only half full.

3. The sun rises at dawn.

4. She has a sore jaw.

5. We saw a goose on the bridge.

6. We will sit on the lawn under the tree.

7. Look at the hawk in the sky.

8. I am sure I saw her in the garden.

9. The hawk has a sharp claw.

10. The dog ate the raw pork.

Dibujos

a. _____

b. _____

c. _____

d. _____

e. _____

f. _____

g. _____

h. _____

i. _____

j. _____

Spelling Dictation * Dictado

Pídale a alguien que le dicte las palabras de la página 30. Después de escribirlas, LÉALAS y revise la ortografía. Corrija las palabras que estén equivocadas.

Fill in the Blanks * Llene el Espacio

Llene cada espacio con una palabra de la lista de palabras. Use cada palabra solamente una vez. Algunas oraciones tienen dibujos al final para ayudarle.

1. He likes to go fishing at _____ .

2. Mom will _____ the pork and then cook it.

3. The boy broke his _____ when he fell.

4. The bugs _____ through the hole in the window.

5. The crab will dig a hole with its _____ .

6. Pam will mow the _____ when it's cooler.

7. I think that ball has a _____.

8. The _____ drank from the pond.

9. He will _____ the ring for cash.

10. The dog put his _____ on the man's lap.

11. Are you _____ you have the tickets?

12. The _____ made a nest in the tall tree.

13. She _____ the kite flying in the sky.

14. The boy will _____ a red flower for his mom.

15. The box is _____ of toy cars and trucks.

Compound Words * Las palabras compuestas

Las palabras compuestas combinan dos palabras pequeñas para formar una palabra. Escriba las dos palabras pequeñas que forman una palabra grande.

Compound Word	Small Word	Small Word
1. everyone	_____	_____
2. something	_____	_____
3. boyfriend	_____	_____
4. playmate	_____	_____
5. milkman	_____	_____
6. paycheck	_____	_____
7. hubcap	_____	_____
8. broomstick	_____	_____
9. hotrod	_____	_____
10. rosebud	_____	_____

Llene los espacios en blanco con una de las palabras compuestas.

11. The witch rides on her _____ .

12. The car's _____ was stolen.

13. Meg's _____ gave her flowers.

14. _____ is busy picking up trash.

15. There is _____ large under the bed.

16. Her _____ is dodging the ball.

17. His _____ is the fastest car in the race.

28

WordSearch * Busca Palabras

Encuentra las palabras de la Lección 5 en el busca palabras. Marca las respuestas. Las palabras pueden estar escritas en forma normal, al revés o diagonalmente.

		draw	**full**
flaw	**lawn**	**crawl**	**saw**

f	j	h	a	w	k	p	s
a	f	a	a	h	a	l	n
w	u	c	w	w	w	p	w
n	l	q	l	a	a	q	a
p	l	h	r	a	w	t	l
b	l	c	e	s	w	a	f
c	w	q	w	a	r	d	s
d	a	w	n	n	w	a	l

Answer Key * Las Respuestas

Sentences * Oraciones (page 26)

a. 8
b. 2
c. 7
d. 1
e. 10

f. 4
g. 3
h. 9
i. 6
j. 5

Spelling Dictation * Dictado (page 26)

catch, slope, draw, broom, show, fudge, locker, want, switch, jaw, crime, playing, snowflake, pledge, standing; Were you on time to catch the bus? Pitch the ball to the catcher.

Fill in the Blanks * Llene el Espacio (page 27)

1. dawn
2. thaw
3. jaw
4. crawl
5. claw
6. lawn
7. flaw
8. fawn

9. pawn
10. paw
11. sure
12. hawk
13. saw
14. draw
15. full

Compound Words * Las palabras compuestas (page 28)

1.	every	one	10.	rose	bud
2.	some	thing	11.	broomstick	
3.	boy	friend	12.	hubcap	
4.	play	mate	13.	boyfriend	
5.	milk	man	14.	Everyone	
6.	pay	check	15.	something	
7.	hub	cap	16.	playmate	
8.	broom	stick	17.	hotrod	
9.	hot	rod			

WordSearch * Busca Palabras (page 29)

f	j	h	a	w	k	p	s
a	f	a	a	h	a	l	n
w	u	c	w	w	p	w
n	l	q	l	a	a	q	a
p	l	h	r	a	w	t	l
b	l	c	e	s	w	a	f
c	w	q	w	a	r	d	s
d	a	w	n	n	w	a	l

Reading and Spelling Check #1
Verificación de lectura y escritura #1

Haga que alguien le dicte las siguientes palabras, leyéndolas por columnas. Escriba las palabras. Cuando haya terminado de escribirlas, léalas. Al pie de esta página, escriba tres veces las palabras que escribió mal. Busque en un diccionario todas las palabras cuyo significado no conozca.

claw	coat	broil	silk
ditch	fudge	catch	notch
melt	crisp	act	would
their	have	corner	tube
slide	trade	drive	resting

Lesson 6 * Lección 6

Word List * La lista de las palabras

Las letras <u>oa</u> suenan como una /o/ larga, como en *boat*. Regla: <u>oa</u> produce el sonido de la <u>o</u> larga y aparece al principio o a la mitad de ciertas palabras cortas.

Inglés	Español
1. boat	bote
2. coat	abrigo
3. road	camino
4. goat	cabra
5. soap	jabón
6. goal	gol
7. toast	pan tostado
8. load	cargar
9. float	flotar
10. oak	roble
11. toad	sapo
12. soak	remojar
13. coast	costa
14. because	porque
15. girl	niña

boat

coat

goat

soap

toast

toad

girl

Sentences * Oraciones

Lea las oraciones. Después escriba el número de la oración debajo del dibujo correcto.

1. The girl will float in the pool.

Dibujos

2. They will sit under the oak tree.

3. The goat ate your math paper.

a. _____

4. We will load the truck with bricks.

b. _____

5. Don't forget to use soap when you shower.

6. The toad sat on the log.

c. _____

7. There are big holes in this road.

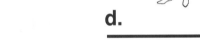

8. Your black coat is hanging in the closet.

d. _____

9. She kicked a goal to win the game.

10. We will have eggs and toast for lunch.

e. _____ f. _____

h. _____

g. _____

i. _____

j. _____

Spelling Dictation * Dictado

Pídale a alguien que le dicte las palabras de la página 37. Después de escribirlas, LÉALAS y revise la ortografía. Corrija las palabras que estén equivocadas.

Fill in the Blanks * Llene el Espacio

Llene cada espacio con una palabra de la lista de palabras. Use cada palabra solamente una vez. Algunas oraciones tienen dibujos al final para ayudarle.

1. The big _____ is slower than the small one.

2. He puts on shorts _____ it is hot.

3. The _____ is too tall to go under the bridge.

4. Let's take the _____ that goes by the river.

5. Dad will _____ his sore foot.

6. The _____ crawled through the window.

7. Tom kicked the last _____ in the game.

8. The _____ jumped from the ledge to the rock.

9. At the _____ they will play in the water.

10. The farmer always hangs his _____ on the peg.

11. The _____ tree has a thick trunk.

12. She likes to _____ on her back.

13. We had _____ with butter and jam.

14. They will _____ the boat with food and drinks.

15. That _____ smells good!

Suffixes * Sufijos

En las palabras monosílabas con una vocal corta seguida de una consonante, la consonante final necesita duplicarse antes de añadir un sufijo vocal (una terminación que comienza con una vocal).

Base Word	Suffixes		
	ing	er	ed
spin	spinning	spinner	spinned

Llene la tabla con cada palabra escrita correctamente.

Base Word	Suffix	New Word
hot	er	1. _____
drip	ing	2. _____
slip	ed	3. _____
thin	er	4. _____
hug	ing	5. _____
stop	ed	6. _____
zip	er	7. _____
clap	ing	8. _____
grab	ed	9. _____

La letra y se usa a menudo como una vocal. Esta regla se aplica cuando se añada una y como sufijo. Llene la tabla con la palabra correcta.

Base Word	Suffix	New Word
fun	y	10. _____
flat	en	11. _____
mud	y	12. _____

WordSearch * Busca Palabras

Encuentra las palabras de la Lección 6 en el busca palabras. Marca las respuestas. Las palabras pueden estar escritas en forma normal, al revés o diagonalmente.

		road	float
goal	load	oak	soak
coast	because		

r	t	v	t	s	a	o	t	c	
g	c	a	k	a	o	s	o	e	
g	i	o	o	h	n	a	s	r	
o	p	r	a	b	t	u	t	o	
a	a	u	l	s	a	m	x	a	
t	o	b	l	c	t	o	y	d	
e	s	a	e	o	k	l	a	k	
d	o	b	l	o	a	d	r	k	
g	w	g	b	t	a	o	l	f	

Answer Key * Las Respuestas

Sentences * Oraciones (page 33)

a.	1	f.	9
b.	10	g.	2
c.	6	h.	4
d.	5	i.	7
e.	8	j.	3

Spelling Dictation * Dictado (page 33)

tube, latch, lawn, soap, brook, clown, judge, smarter, road, says, patch, swipe, resting, raincoat, badge; Hitch the trailer to the camper. He rode his bike under the bridge.

Fill in the Blanks * Llene el Espacio (page 34)

1.	goat	9.	coast
2.	because	10.	coat
3.	boat	11.	oak
4.	road	12.	float
5.	soak	13.	toast
6.	girl	14.	load
7.	goal	15.	soap
8.	toad		

Suffixes * Sufijos (page 35)

1.	hotter	7.	zipper
2.	dripping	8.	clapping
3.	slipped	9.	grabbed
4.	thinner	10.	funny
5.	hugging	11.	flatten
6.	stopped	12.	muddy

WordSearch * Busca Palabras (page 36)

Lesson 7 * Lección 7

Word List * Lista de palabras

Las letras <u>oi</u> se pronuncian /oi/, como en *boil*. Regla: <u>oi</u> aparece al principio o a la mitad de una palabra. Las letras <u>oy</u> producen el mismo sonido pero aparecen al final de una palabra.

Inglés	Español
1. boil	hervir
2. coin	moneda
3. spoil	echarse a perder
4. moist	húmedo
5. join	reunir
6. oil	aceite
7. soil	suelo
8. joint	articulación
9. broil	asar
10. point	señalar
11. boy	niño
12. toy	juguete
13. enjoy	disfrutar
14. where	dónde
15. wear	tener puesto

boil

coin

oil

soil

boy

Sentences * Oraciones

Lea las oraciones. Después escriba el número de la oración debajo del dibujo correcto.

1. The girl points to the hawk in the sky.

2. The pork will spoil in the sun.

3. She will put oil in her car.

4. After the rain, the soil is very moist.

5. Sam will boil the water.

6. His joint is sore.

7. Let's join the tennis club.

8. We will wear long pants.

9. He enjoys making fudge.

10. That coin is from Mexico.

Dibujos

a. _____

b. _____

c. _____

d. _____

e. _____

f. _____

g. _____

h. _____

i. _____

j. _____

Spelling Dictation * Dictado

Pídale a alguien que le dicte las palabras de la página 43. Después de escribirlas, LÉALAS y revise la ortografía. Corrija las palabras que estén equivocadas.

Fill in the Blank * Llene el Espacio

Llene cada espacio con una palabra de la lista de palabras. Use cada palabra solamente una vez. Algunas oraciones tienen dibujos al final para ayudarle.

1. The big ship had an _____ spill.

2. _____ is the black patch for Tom's pants?

3. This _____ is playing with the goats.

4. They will _____ the club at the lodge.

5. The farmer will _____ the milk.

6. Dad plans to _____ the chicken.

7. The soil is too _____ to plant the flowers.

8. Please do not _____ your finger at me.

9. We _____ flying the small plane.

10. She will plant flowers in the rich _____ .

11. Meg will _____ a dress when she goes shopping.

12. Her _____ is sore from playing too much tennis.

13. The rich man owns a rare _____ .

14. That _____ has sharp edges.

15. The milk will _____ in the sun.

40

Adding s or es to Words that End in y
Cómo añadir s o es a palabras que terminan en y

Cuando añada s a palabras que terminan en y, debe cambiar la y a i y luego añadir es si la y está precedida de una consonante. Si la y está precedida de una vocal, sólo añada una s. La pronunciación de la s será de todos modos un sonido /z/.

Original Word	Add es	Original Word	Add s
cry	cries	pay	pays
fly	flies	toy	toys

Llene los espacios en blanco con las palabras a continuación. Añada s a cada palabra, siguiendo las reglas anteriores.

dry	play	buy	try
boy	say	spy	enjoy
day	fry	ray	spray

1. The small girl _____ playing at the park.

2. The boy _____ his dog with water.

3. Mom _____ a tan raincoat.

4. The warm _____ from the sun feel good.

5. The boy _____ with the toad on the lawn.

6. Sam _____ his hands on his shorts.

7. The farmer _____ the flowers will bloom in two weeks.

8. The _____ are longer in spring than in winter.

9. The man stands under the bridge and _____ on the two men.

10. The _____ are picking plums.

11. He _____ three eggs for lunch.

12. She _____ to catch the fast ball.

41

WordSearch * Busca Palabras

Encuentra las palabras de la Lección 7 en el busca palabras. Marca las respuestas. Las palabras pueden estar escritas en forma normal, al revés o diagonalmente.

	moist	**join**	**joint**
broil	**point**	**wear**	**toy**
enjoy	**spoil**		

j	n	p	o	i	n	t	d	n
l	o	i	r	a	e	w	i	l
l	p	i	o	m	v	o	i	l
s	i	y	n	c	j	o	i	m
p	y	o	o	t	b	o	r	o
o	x	b	s	j	r	o	u	q
i	n	y	y	b	n	p	i	a
l	o	o	t	z	c	e	w	l
t	b	m	o	i	s	t	i	e

Answer Key * Las Respuestas

Sentences * Oraciones (page 39)

a.	2	f.	3	
b.	4	g.	7	
c.	6	h.	1	
d.	9	i.	8	
e.	5	j.	10	

Spelling Dictation * Dictado (page 39)

brave, notch, claw, coin, tooth, frowning, wedge, farmer, toast, where, batch, saw, frame, blinking, windmill; Dad made a batch of fudge. They said the pledge to the flag.

Fill in the Blank * Llene el Espacio (page 40)

1.	oil	9.	enjoy	
2.	Where	10.	soil	
3.	boy	11.	wear	
4.	join	12.	joint	
5.	boil	13.	coin	
6.	broil	14.	toy	
7.	moist	15.	spoil	
8.	point			

Adding s to Words that End in y * Cómo añadir s a palabras que terminan en y (page 41)

1.	enjoys	7.	says
2.	sprays	8.	days
3.	buys	9.	spies
4.	rays	10.	boys
5.	plays	11.	fries
6.	dries	12.	tries

WordSearch * Busca Palabras (page 42)

Lesson 8 * Lección 8

Word List * Lista de palabras

En esta lista, la letra <u>c</u> se pronuncia /s/, como en *nice*. Regla: La letra <u>c</u> produce el sonido /s/ cuando la sigue una <u>e</u>, <u>i</u>, o <u>y</u>.

Inglés	Español
1. nice	agradable
2. place	poner
3. rice	arroz
4. race	carrera
5. face	cara
6. mice	ratones
7. price	precio
8. spice	especia
9. center	centro
10. cent	centavo
11. ice	hielo
12. slice	rebanada
13. there	hay
14. their	su
15. they're	ellos están

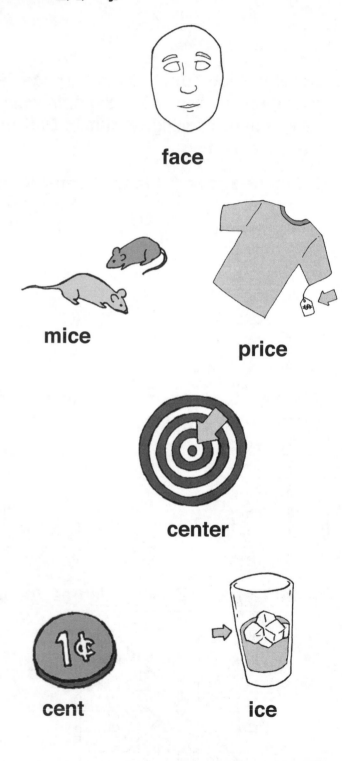

face

mice

price

center

cent

ice

44

Sentences * Oraciones

Lea las oraciones. Después escriba el número de la oración debajo del dibujo correcto.

1. The mice are in the center of the maze.

2. Do you want ice in your coke?

3. The girl won the race.

4. Would you like a slice of cake?

5. They're playing in the rain.

6. The price of the toy is ten cents.

7. Their dog is growling at us.

8. He has a scar on his face.

9. There is a parking place under the tree.

10. Dad will boil the rice.

Dibujos

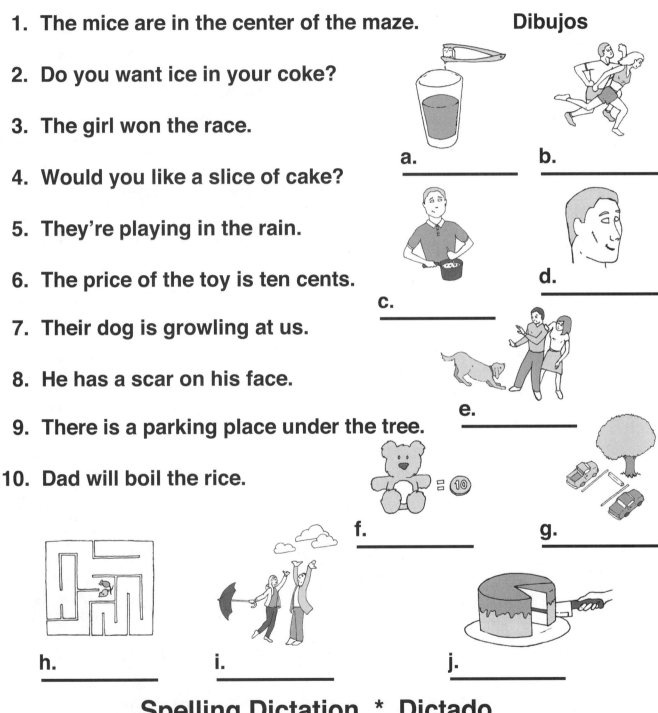

a. _____

b. _____

c. _____

d. _____

e. _____

f. _____

g. _____

h. _____

i. _____

j. _____

Spelling Dictation * Dictado

Pídale a alguien que le dicte las palabras de la página 49. Después de escribirlas, LÉALAS y revise la ortografía. Corrija las palabras que estén equivocadas.

45

Fill in the Blank * Llene el Espacio

Llene cada espacio con una palabra de la lista de palabras. Use cada palabra solamente una vez. Algunas oraciones tienen dibujos al final para ayudarle.

1. The gum costs one _____ .

2. _____ busy painting the lodge.

3. Ted is a _____ boy.

4. _____ needs a lot of water to grow.

5. The _____ ran under the bed.

6. _____ is oil on your pants.

7. The _____ will keep the milk from spoiling.

8. We saw the red car win the _____ .

9. He painted his _____ red and white.

10. Where should I _____ the books?

11. _____ pink flowers bloom every spring.

12. Mom is sitting in the _____ of the room.

13. What _____ did you put in the rice?

14. The small girl wants a thick _____ of ham.

15. What is the _____ of the black coat?

Noun or Verb * Sustantivo o Verbo

En cada oración, la palabra subrayada es un sustantivo o un verbo. Un sustantivo nombra a una persona, una criatura, un lugar o una cosa. Un verbo es una palabra de acción. Después de cada oración escriba *verb* (verbo) o *noun* (sustantivo) dependiendo de cómo se use la palabra subrayada. La primera oración ya se ha hecho.

1. Please <u>hook</u> the trailer to the van.　　　*verb*

2. Please hang your coat on the <u>hook</u>.　　　_____

3. Mom <u>cooks</u> eggs and ham for lunch.　　　_____

4. The <u>cooks</u> wear big white hats.　　　_____

5. She <u>drinks</u> milk for dinner.　　　_____

6. The cold <u>drinks</u> are on the mat.　　　_____

7. The dishes are in the <u>sink</u>.　　　_____

8. The rocks <u>sink</u> in the water.　　　_____

9. The <u>slide</u> in the park is wet.　　　_____

10. They <u>slide</u> down the hill on a big sled.　　　_____

11. The bells <u>ring</u> at ten.　　　_____

12. She lost her <u>ring</u> at the fair.　　　_____

13. At the park, he likes to play on the <u>swings</u>.　　　_____

14. He <u>swings</u> the bat and gets a hit.　　　_____

WordSearch * Busca Palabras

Encuentra las palabras de la Lección 8 en el busca palabras. Marca las respuestas. Las palabras pueden estar escritas en forma normal, al revés o diagonalmente.

		race	place
spice	rice	slice	nice
there	their		

t	e	d	e	c	a	r	f	c
s	n	c	q	b	z	a	e	e
l	e	e	i	v	c	n	c	t
i	t	c	c	e	t	i	e	h
c	h	c	a	e	n	q	c	e
e	e	u	r	l	m	l	i	i
g	r	u	d	a	p	i	r	r
t	e	e	c	i	p	s	c	n
v	h	t	e	c	i	r	p	e

Answer Key * Las Respuestas

Sentences * Oraciones (page 45)

a. 2	f. 6
b. 3	g. 9
c. 10	h. 1
d. 8	i. 5
e. 7	j. 4

Spelling Dictation * Dictado (page 45)

lime, claw, roost, face, would, growling, boat, give, boil, stitch, place, blade, foam, yawn, ledge; Tom has to mow the lawn. She will toss three coins into the pool.

Fill in the Blank * Llene el Espacio (page 46)

1. cent	9. face
2. They're	10. place
3. nice	11. Their
4. Rice	12. center
5. mice	13. spice
6. There	14. slice
7. ice	15. price
8. race	

Noun or Verb * Sustantivo o Verbo (page 47)

1. verb	8. verb
2. noun	9. noun
3. verb	10. verb
4. noun	11. verb
5. verb	12. noun
6. noun	13. noun
7. noun	14. verb

WordSearch * Busca Palabras (page 48)

Lesson 9 * Lección 9

Word List * Lista de palabras

En esta lista, la letra g se pronuncia /j/, como en *page*. Regla: La letra g produce el sonido /j/ cuando la sigue una e, i, or y.

Inglés	Español
1. cage	jaula
2. age	edad
3. page	página
4. large	grande
5. germ	germen
6. gem	gema
7. fringe	fleco
8. barge	barcaza
9. stage	escenario
10. rage	furia
11. hinge	bisagra
12. plunge	meter
13. to	a
14. two	dos
15. too	demasiado

cage

gem

fringe

barge

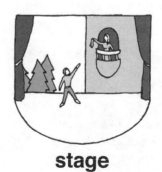

stage

hinge

Sentences * Oraciones

Lea las oraciones. Después escriba el número de la oración debajo del dibujo correcto.

1. Her ring has a large gem.

2. The hinge on the door is broken.

3. The kids will plunge into the water.

4. The small tugboat pulled the barge.

5. There is pink fringe on the bottom of her dress.

6. We will lock the mice in the cage.

7. The two goats ate the farmer's corn.

8. She stood on the stage and sang a long song.

9. The dog growled at the large hawk.

10. She put five stickers on the page.

Dibujos

a. —————————

b. —————————

c. —————————

d. —————————

e. —————————

f. —————————

g. —————————

h. —————————

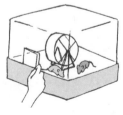

i. —————————

j. —————————

Spelling Dictation * Dictado

Pídale a alguien que le dicte las palabras de la página 55. Después de escribirlas, LÉALAS y revise la ortografía. Corrija las palabras que estén equivocadas.

Fill in the Blanks * Llene el Espacio

Llene cada espacio con una palabra de la lista de palabras. Use cada palabra solamente una vez. Algunas oraciones tienen dibujos al final para ayudarle.

1. The _____ is full of oil.

2. She spilled milk on the _____.

3. He ring has a large red _____.?

4. He ate _____ much fudge.

5. The boy runs _____ his mom.

6. There is a _____ cow standing in the road.

7. Please fix the _____ on the small wooden box.

8. The frogs _____ into the pond.

9. The _____ is too small to see.

10. She wants the boots with the white _____.

11. What is your _____ ?

12. At _____ o'clock we will go to the store.

13. The latch on the _____ is broken.

14. That tall thin boy is full of _____.

15. The girl will sing a song on the _____.

52

Noun or Verb * Sustantivo o Verbo

En cada oración, la palabra subrayada es un sustantivo o un verbo. Un sustantivo nombra a una persona, una criatura, un lugar o una cosa. Un verbo es una palabra de acción. Después de cada oración escriba *verb* (verbo) o *noun* (sustantivo) dependiendo de cómo se use la palabra subrayada. La primera oración ya se ha hecho.

1. Meg swats the <u>flies</u> off the cake.   *noun*

2. Meg <u>flies</u> a small plane. _____

3. The <u>spies</u> are wearing tan raincoats. _____

4. He <u>spies</u> on his big sister. _____

5. She <u>drops</u> the large glass of water. _____

6. There are <u>drops</u> of water on the silk dress. _____

7. They <u>check</u> their math pages. _____

8. The <u>check</u> is in the mail. _____

9. The rich man has a tall <u>stack</u> of bills. _____

10. Please <u>stack</u> the boxes in the corner. _____

11. They <u>show</u> us their large boat. _____

12. The <u>show</u> will begin at ten. _____

13. They put a fresh coat of <u>paint</u> on the wall. _____

14. They will <u>paint</u> the fence green. _____

WordSearch * Busca Palabras

Encuentra las palabras de la Lección 9 en el busca palabras. Marca las respuestas. Las palabras pueden estar escritas en forma normal, al revés o diagonalmente.

		page	large
germ	age	rage	plunge
to	two	too	

m	m	h	i	n	g	e	e	h
z	r	e	z	j	h	g	e	e
e	p	e	g	g	a	g	g	s
g	t	e	g	c	n	a	e	t
r	n	y	g	u	p	i	c	a
a	c	o	l	n	r	o	k	g
b	o	p	e	x	i	a	w	e
t	o	g	y	d	g	r	g	t
t	a	e	g	r	a	l	f	e

Answer Key * Las Respuestas

Sentences * Oraciones (page 51)

a. 2

b. 5

c. 3

d. 8

e. 7

f. 1

g. 9

h. 6

i. 4

j. 10

Spelling Dictation * Dictado (page 51)

fine, raw, soon, ice, could, showing, goat, page, have, coil, match, hope, boast, draw, large; Meg can kick the ball past the goal. Plant the seeds in the moist, black soil.

Fill in the Blanks * Llene el Espacio (page 52)

1. barge

2. page

3. gem

4. too

5. to

6. large

7. hinge

8. plunge

9. germ

10. fringe

11. age

12. two

13. cage

14. rage

15. stage

Noun or Verb * Sustantivo o Verbo (page 53)

1.	noun	8.	noun
2.	verb	9.	noun
3.	noun	10.	verb
4.	verb	11.	verb
5.	verb	12.	noun
6.	noun	13.	noun
7.	verb	14.	verb

WordSearch * Busca Palabras (page 54)

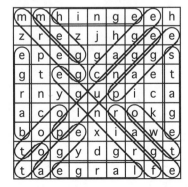

Lesson 10 * Lección 10

Word List * Lista de palabras

Las letras <u>ea</u> suenan como una /e/ larga, como en *eat*. Las letras <u>ea</u> son un equipo de vocales. A menudo la primera vocal en un equipo de vocales dirá su nombre y la segunda vocal es muda. No hay diferencia de sonido entre <u>ea</u> y <u>ee</u>.

Inglés	Español
1. eat	comer
2. tea	té
3. beach	playa
4. reach	alcanzar
5. teacher	maestra
6. east	este
7. meal	comida
8. dream	sueño
9. team	equipo
10. seal	foca
11. read	leer
12. meat	carne
13. heal	sanar
14. meet	encontrarse
15. heel	talón

beach

teacher

meal

team

seal

read

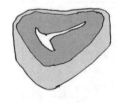

meat

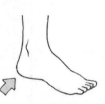

heel

Sentences * Oraciones

Lea las oraciones. Después escriba el número de la oración debajo del dibujo correcto.

1. The sun rises in the east.

2. This cream will heal your cut.

3. Let's eat lunch under the tree.

4. Dad cooked a big meal for the kids.

5. Would you like milk or tea with your cake?

6. The seal swims at the beach.

7. Mom will cook the meat on the grill.

8. Can you reach the cage on the top shelf?

9. He will put a bandage on his heel.

10. She will read a book at the beach.

Dibujos

a. _____

b. _____

c. _____

d. _____

e. _____

f. _____

g. _____

h. _____

i. _____

j. _____

Spelling Dictation * Dictado

Pídale a alguien que le dicte las palabras de la página 61. Después de escribirlas, LÉALAS y revise la ortografía. Corrija las palabras que estén equivocadas.

Fill in the Blank * Llene el Espacio

Llene cada espacio con una palabra de la lista de palabras. Use cada palabra solamente una vez. Algunas oraciones tienen dibujos al final para ayudarle.

1. I am full after that big _____ .

2. I will drink _____ with my lunch.

3. We will meet the _____ after class.

4. Please _____ under the sink and get the soap.

5. There is a large _____ swimming under the dock.

6. We live on the _____ side of town.

7. My left _____ is very sore.

8. You may get sick if you _____ raw meat.

9. The _____ will play basketball at the park.

10. Let's _____ at five o'clock to play chess.

11. I like to _____ books about flowers.

12. I hope this cream will _____ your sore joint.

13. Cut the _____ into thin slices.

14. The small boy woke up from a bad _____ .

15. Let's play volleyball at the _____ .

Contractions * Contracciones

En español solamente hay dos contracciones: *del* (de + el) y *al* (al + el). En inglés son muy comunes. Se juntan dos palabras omitiendo una o dos letras. Se pone un apóstrofe donde se omiten las letras.

Escriba una oración con cada una de las contracciones de la tabla.

Words	Contraction	Words	Contraction
I will	I'll	I have	I've
you will	you'll	you have	you've
he will	he'll	we have	we've
she will	she'll	I would	I'd
we will	we'll	we would	we'd

1. _____

2. _____

3. _____

4. _____

5. _____

6. _____

7. _____

8. _____

9. _____

10. _____

WordSearch * Busca Palabras

Encuentra las palabras de la Lección 10 en el busca palabras. Marca las respuestas. Las palabras pueden estar escritas en forma normal, al revés o diagonalmente.

			reach
east	dream	team	eat
meet	heal		tea

d	h	y	h	c	a	e	r	l
r	r	e	l	a	e	s	e	e
l	e	e	a	j	s	e	a	c
h	a	h	a	l	h	s	e	d
o	t	e	c	m	t	b	e	a
t	e	d	m	a	e	a	x	e
e	a	q	e	a	e	c	e	r
e	m	a	c	m	i	t	z	t
m	t	h	m	e	a	t	w	l

Answer Key * Las Respuestas

Sentences * Oraciones (page 57)

a. 7

b. 3

c. 5

d. 8

e. 10

f. 1

g. 6

h. 9

i. 2

j. 4

Spelling Dictation * Dictado (57)

hive, claw, stoop, reach, clown, mice, should, dance, seat, clutch, drove, rage, soap, judge, joint; Stand by the fence and look at the seal. She has a very huge gem in her ring.

Fill in the Blank * Llene el Espacio (page 58)

1. meal

2. tea

3. teacher

4. reach

5. seal

6. east

7. heel

8. eat

9. team

10. meet

11. read

12. heal

13. meat

14. dream

15. beach

Contractions * Contracciones (page 59)

1. – 10. Answers will vary.

WordSearch * Busca Palabras (page 60)

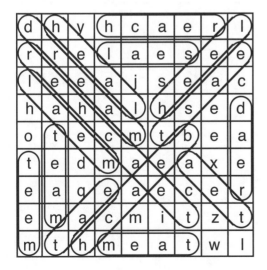

Reading and Spelling Check #2
Verificación de lectura y escritura #2

Haga que alguien le dicte las siguientes palabras, leyéndolas por columnas. Escriba las palabras. Cuando haya terminado de escribirlas, léalas. Al pie de esta página, escriba tres veces las palabras que escribió mal. Busque en un diccionario todas las palabras cuyo significado no conozca.

thaw	cloak	broil	milk
hitch	ledge	match	toast
coin	page	bribe	should
were	want	teacher	cube
mile	place	fork	looking

Lesson 11 * Lección 11

Word List * Lista de palabras

Las letras <u>ew</u> se pronuncian /oo/, como en *new*. La forma <u>ew</u> es la opción preferida para escribir el sonido /oo/ al final de una palabra.

Inglés	Español
1. new	nuevo
2. blew	sopló
3. few	pocos
4. grew	creció
5. chew	masticar
6. stew	estofado
7. dew	rocío
8. drew	dibujó
9. crew	tripulación
10. flew	voló
11. pew	banco
12. one	uno
13. won	ganó
14. by	junto a
15. buy	comprar

stew

dew

drew

pew

one

Sentences * Oraciones

Lea las oraciones. Después escriba el número de la oración debajo del dibujo correcto.

1. The wind blew the pages off the ledge.

2. He has a new fishing pole.

3. There are only a few cupcakes left.

4. The hawk flew to the top of the roof.

5. The sunflower grew very tall.

6. They will sit on the long pew.

7. He drew a flower for his mother.

8. Every morning there is dew on the grass.

9. Meg's horse won the race.

10. She cooked the stew in the large pot.

Dibujos

a. _____

b. _____

c. _____

d. _____

e. _____

f. _____

g. _____

h. _____

i. _____

j. _____

Spelling Dictation * Dictado

Pídale a alguien que le dicte las palabras de la página 68. Después de escribirlas, LÉALAS y revise la ortografía. Corrija las palabras que estén equivocadas.

Fill in the Blank * Llene el Espacio

Llene cada espacio con una palabra de la lista de palabras. Use cada palabra solamente una vez. Algunas oraciones tienen dibujos al final para ayudarle.

1. She sat on the hard _____ for a long time.

2. I will _____ a new coat today.

3. Please _____ your food well.

5. There is meat, corn, and peas in the _____ .

5. We will meet _____ the big oak tree.

6. We have a _____ teacher for our math class.

7. Her fudge _____ fourth place.

8. The ship's _____ was busy all day.

9. He _____ a map of the farm.

10. The boy _____ out the match.

11. Only a _____ of the roses are blooming.

12. The farmer's corn _____ tall.

13. Our boots are wet from the _____ .

14. The plane _____ low over the lake.

15. There is only _____ car in the parking lot.

Contractions * Contracciones

En español solamente hay dos contracciones: *del* (de + el) y *al* (al + el). En inglés son muy comunes. Se juntan dos palabras omitiendo una o dos letras. Se pone un apóstrofe donde se omiten las letras.

Escriba una oración con cada una de las contracciones de la tabla.

Words	Contraction	Words	Contraction
are not	aren't	do not	don't
did not	didn't	I am	I'm
would not	wouldn't	you are	you're
could not	couldn't	we are	we're
should not	shouldn't	they are	they're

1. _____

2. _____

3. _____

4. _____

5. _____

6. _____

7. _____

8. _____

9. _____

10. _____

WordSearch * Busca Palabras

Encuentra las palabras de la Lección 11 en el busca palabras. Marca las respuestas. Las palabras pueden estar escritas en forma normal, al revés o diagonalmente.

1	blew	flew	grew
chew	crew	few	new
won	by	buy	

c	n	f	g	r	e	w	d
w	r	u	e	y	z	e	w
b	o	e	c	w	w	e	h
y	w	n	w	h	l	y	w
i	x	w	d	b	e	c	e
o	e	r	w	e	y	w	l
p	e	e	w	u	n	u	f
w	n	s	t	e	w	o	b

Answer Key * Las Respuestas

Sentences * Oraciones (page 64)

a. 4

b. 6

c. 10

d. 7

e. 5

f. 2

g. 1

h. 3

i. 9

j. 8

Spelling Dictation * Dictado (page 64)

fire, jaw, wool, team, crowd, lace, flew, very, barge, read, ditch, mule, cage, float, chew; He drew a map of the lodge. The kids will plunge into the cool water.

Fill in the Blank * Llene el Espacio (page 65)

1. pew

2. buy

3. chew

4. stew

5. by

6. new

7. won

8. crew

9. drew

10. blew

11. few

12. grew

13. dew

14. flew

15. one

Contractions * Contracciones (page 66)

1.-10. Answers will vary.

WordSearch * Busca Palabras (page 67)

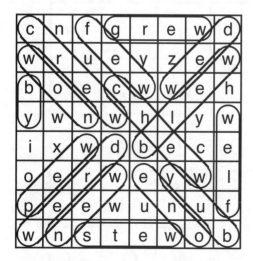

Lesson 12 * Lección 12

Word List * Lista de palabras

En esta lista, <u>ear</u> se pronuncia /ear/, como en *hear*.

Inglés	Español
1. hear	escuchar
2. ear	oído
3. near	cerca
4. dear	querido
5. fear	temor
6. tear	lágrima
7. clear	claro
8. spear	lanza
9. year	año
10. gear	engranaje
11. shear	esquilar
12. we're	estamos
13. were	estaban
14. are	están
15. our	nuestro

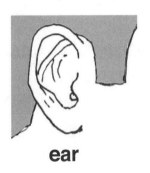

ear

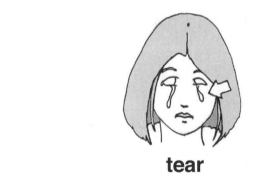

tear

spear

Sentences * Oraciones

Lea las oraciones. Después escriba el número de la oración debajo del dibujo correcto.

1. The farmer will shear the sheep.

2. The tear ran down the small girl's face.

3. I will buy the large spear for my dad.

4. He is patching the bike's tire.

5. Our boat has a large yellow sail.

6. A bee stung her ear.

7. The plates are near the pot of stew.

8. The boys were looking at the seals.

9. We're going to swim at the pool.

10. I can hear the dog barking.

Dibujos

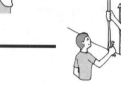

a. _____

b. _____

c. _____

d. _____

e. _____

f. _____

g. _____

h. _____

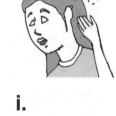

i. _____

j. _____

Spelling Dictation * Dictado

Pídale a alguien que le dicte las palabras de la página 74. Después de escribirlas, LÉALAS y revise la ortografía. Corrija las palabras que estén equivocadas.

Fill in the Blank * Llene el Espacio

Llene cada espacio con una palabra de la lista de palabras. Use cada palabra solamente una vez. Algunas oraciones tienen dibujos al final para ayudarle.

1. I do not hear well out of my left _____ .

2. _____ enjoying the sunshine.

3. Last _____ we trudged through deep snow.

6. I did not _____ the bell for class.

5. A _____ on my bike is broken.

6. Tom hung the _____ in his bedroom.

7. _____ team won the race.

8. Where _____ you yesterday?

9. The air is very _____ today.

10. We _____ reading books in the backyard.

11. We live _____ the beach.

12. A big _____ rolled down her cheek.

13. The boy feels _____ when he sees the large dog.

14. We are visiting our _____ friend who is ill.

15. He will _____ the wool off the sheep.

Base Words * Palabras base

Una palabra base es la palabra antes de añadir afijo alguno. Escriba la palabra base de cada una de las palabras a continuación. La primera palabra ya se ha escrito para usted.

Word	Base Word
making	1. _____ make _____
plunged	2. _____
slipping	3. _____
crawls	4. _____
soaked	5. _____
pledging	6. _____
stretched	7. _____
hatches	8. _____
hiking	9. _____
running	10. _____
pointing	11. _____
dresses	12. _____

Sight Word Practice
Práctica con palabras de lectura automática

Las palabras de lectura automática son palabras comunes que a menudo no siguen las reglas. Estas palabras deben escribirse correctamente porque se usan a menudo.

Elimine una letra en cada palabra para formar una nueva palabra.

Sight Word	New Word
what	13. _____ hat _____
they	14. _____
two	15. _____
one	16. _____
knew	17. _____
many	18. _____
want	19. _____
buy	20. _____
where	21. _____
know	22. _____
said	23. _____

WordSearch * Busca Palabras

Encuentra las palabras de la Lección 12 en el busca palabras. Marca las respuestas. Las palabras pueden estar escritas en forma normal, al revés o diagonalmente.

	hear	near	
dear	fear	clear	gear
shear	are	were	our

t	f	e	r	a	e	p	s
e	e	r	h	e	a	r	e
a	a	c	a	m	h	r	a
r	r	e	l	e	a	s	v
r	x	f	b	e	h	g	r
a	l	n	o	e	a	x	a
e	z	u	a	o	m	r	e
d	r	r	n	e	a	r	g

Answer Key * Las Respuestas

Sentences * Oraciones (page 70)

a. 10
b. 3
c. 7
d. 2
e. 9

f. 4
g. 5
h. 1
i. 6
j. 8

Spelling Dictation * Dictado (page 70)

whale, fawn, book, team, show, face, grew, prince, catch, cube, sage, coach, chew, dodge, broil; I like the fringe on your boots. Tom got on the stage to sing.

Fill in the Blank * Llene el Espacio (page 71)

1. ear
2. We're
3. year
4. hear
5. gear
6. spear
7. Our
8. were

9. clear
10. are
11. near
12. tear
13. fear
14. dear
15. shear

Base words and Sight Word Practice * Práctica con palabras de lectura automática (page 72)

1. make	9. hike	17. new
2. plunge	10. run	18. man
3. slip	11. point	19. ant
4. crawl	12. dress	20. by
5. soak	13. hat	21. here
6. pledge	14. the	22. now
7. stretch	15. to	23. aid
8. hatch	16. on	

WordSearch * Busca Palabras (page 73)

74

Lesson 13 * Lección 13

Word List * Lista de palabras

Las letras <u>igh</u> pronuncian el sonido largo /i/, como en *night*. Las letras <u>igh</u> están generalmente al final de una palabra o las sigue la letra <u>t</u>.

Inglés	Español
1. high	elevado
2. night	noche
3. right	derecho
4. fight	pelea
5. bright	brillante
6. light	luz
7. tight	estrecho
8. fighting	peleando
9. brighter	más brillante
10. tighter	mas estrecho
11. would	verbo auxiliar
12. wood	madera
13. knew	sabía
14. new	nuevo

night

fight   fighting

wood

75

Sentences * Oraciones

Lea las oraciones. Después escriba el número de la oración debajo del dibujo correcto.

1. Can you reach up high to get the box?

2. The sun is bright on a clear day.

3. At night owls look for food.

5. The two boys got into a fight.

5. The new pants are too tight.

6. We will light the wood with a match.

7. Would you please close the window?

8. This bulb will be brighter.

9. Put the coins in your right hand.

10. The big box is lighter than the small box.

Dibujos

a. _____

b. _____

c. _____

d. _____

e. _____

f. _____

g. _____

h. _____

i. _____

j. _____

Spelling Dictation * Dictado

Pídale a alguien que le dicte las palabras de la página 80. Después de escribirlas, LÉALAS y revise la ortografía. Corrija las palabras que estén equivocadas.

76

Fill in the Blank * Llene el Espacio

Llene cada espacio con una palabra de la lista de palabras. Use cada palabra solamente una vez. Algunas oraciones tienen dibujos al final para ayudarle.

1. The boys were _____ in the park.

2. The _____ chair is in the bedroom.

3. The price for that coat is too _____ .

7. At _____ , we can see many stars in the sky.

5. He painted his car _____ red.

6. Please switch on the _____ .

7. Please whisper the name in my _____ ear.

8. The men _____ how to fix the hinge.

9. _____ you like to go to the beach with us?

10. Please stack the _____ in the corner.

11. The red dress is _____ than the black one.

12. It is _____ when the shades are up.

13. The teacher stopped the _____ .

14. Those jeans are too _____ for you.

Sight Words * Palabras de lectura automática

Las siguientes son palabras comunes que no siguen las reglas de deletreo.

of	to	your	do
they	friend	from	what
were	where	any	water

Use las palabras mira una vez para llenar los espacios en blanco.

1. _____ you know that teacher?

2. Your _____ is on the baseball team.

3. Are there _____ mice in the barn?

4. They _____ done painting by noon.

5. Would you like a glass _____ milk?

6. The kids will jump in the _____ .

7. _____ did you put in the stew?

8. The gift is _____ your best friend.

9. _____ will light the fire with a match.

10. _____ did you put the soap?

11. Last night we went _____ the store.

12. _____ book is on the top shelf.

WordSearch * Busca Palabras

Encuentra las palabras de la Lección 13 en el busca palabras. Marca las respuestas. Las palabras pueden estar escritas en forma normal, al revés o diagonalmente.

		bright	
high	right	light	brighter
tight	tighter		would
knew	new		

h	d	t	h	g	i	t	w	t	l
f	g	o	o	i	f	e	g	i	s
m	b	i	o	p	n	n	g	r	r
t	u	r	h	w	i	h	l	i	e
h	o	c	i	t	t	v	r	g	t
g	t	g	h	g	f	w	y	h	h
i	k	g	w	x	h	i	c	t	g
n	i	e	d	d	c	t	g	q	i
f	n	w	o	u	l	d	e	h	t
k	b	r	i	g	h	t	n	r	t

Answer Key * Las Respuestas

Sentences * Oraciones (page 76)

a.	7	f.	9
b.	4	g.	1
c.	2	h.	5
d.	3	i.	8
e.	6	j.	10

Spelling Dictation * Dictado (page 76)

price, right, paw, beach, grew, race, where, reach, hitch, bright, spice, large, soap, bridge, chew; The cook put pork in the stew. Meg hit a high ball in baseball.

Fill in the Blank * Llene el Espacio (page 77)

1.	fighting	8.	knew
2.	lighter	9.	Would
3.	high	10.	wood
4.	night	11.	tighter
5.	bright	12.	brighter
6.	light	13.	fight
7.	right	14.	tight

Sight Words * Palabras de lectura automática (page 78)

1.	Do	7.	What
2.	friend	8.	from
3.	any	9.	They
4.	were	10.	Where
5.	of	11.	to
6.	water	12.	Your

WordSearch * Busca Palabras (page 79)

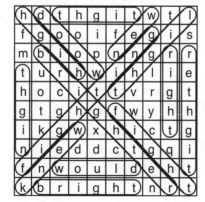

80

Lesson 14 * Lección 14

Word List * Lista de palabras

Las letras <u>ou</u> se pronuncian /ou/, como en <u>house</u>. Regla: <u>ou</u> es la opción de preferencia para este sonido en la mitad de una palabra.

Inglés	Español
1. house	casa
2. mouse	ratón
3. mouth	boca
4. found	encontró
5. south	sur
6. round	redondo
7. cloud	nube
8. sound	sonido
9. loud	fuerte
10. out	fuera
11. count	contar
12. shout	gritar
13. flour	harina
14. our	nuestro

house

mouse

cloud

flour

Sentences * Oraciones

Lea las oraciones. Después escriba el número de la oración debajo del dibujo correcto.

1. We found the flashlight under the bed.

2. Please chew with your mouth closed.

3. I hear a mouse in the corner.

6. He has a very round face.

5. Their house is on the right.

6. She blew out the match.

7. Our team won the game.

8. I hear a loud sound in the boy's bedroom.

9. He will use flour to make the cake.

10. Please do not shout in my ear.

Dibujos

a. _____

b. _____

c. _____

d. _____

f. _____

e. _____

g. _____

h. _____

i. _____

j. _____

Spelling Dictation * Dictado

Pídale a alguien que le dicte las palabras de la página 86. Después de escribirlas, LÉALAS y revise la ortografía. Corrija las palabras que estén equivocadas.

Fill in the Blank * Llene el Espacio

Llene cada espacio con una palabra de la lista de palabras. Use cada palabra solamente una vez. Algunas oraciones tienen dibujos al final para ayudarle.

1. The _____ is on the top shelf.

2. The small girl can _____ to one hundred.

3. The bug flew in his _____ .

4. You may _____ on the playground.

5. That _____ looks like a seal.

6. We will meet at the _____ end of the beach.

7. Did you hear that _____ boom last night?

8. The small white _____ will eat the cheese.

9. He _____ his toy spear under the tree.

10. What is making that hissing _____ ?

11. _____ car is stuck in the mud.

12. Please take _____ the trash.

13. We will meet at your _____ .

14. The girl made a _____ cake with two layers.

Sight Words * Palabras de lectura automática

Las siguientes son palabras comunes que no siguen las reglas de deletreo.

want	was	come	some
many	been	could	there
their	are	one	said

Use las palabras mira una vez para llenar los espacios en blanco.

1. How _____ mice are in the cage?

2. We need _____ matches to light the fire.

3. They _____ stew and milk for lunch.

4. _____ house is the big one on the hill.

5. Where _____ we going?

6. They will _____ to the beach at ten o'clock.

7. There is only _____ boat at the dock.

8. My mom _____ I could go with you.

9. _____ is a mouse under the chair.

10. We have _____ busy this year.

11. _____ you come at noon?

12. Last night he _____ counting his coins.

WordSearch * Busca Palabras

Encuentra las palabras de la Lección 14 en el busca palabras. Marca las respuestas. Las palabras pueden estar escritas en forma normal, al revés o diagonalmente.

mouth	**found**	**round**	**loud**
out	**our**	**count**	**shout**

j	k	t	d	d	m	u	i	s
n	u	u	n	t	v	u	n	h
o	o	u	n	e	z	j	f	o
l	o	u	e	r	s	r	m	u
f	o	n	c	c	u	u	u	t
c	h	b	t	a	l	o	o	o
n	d	n	u	o	r	o	l	h
m	o	u	t	h	f	u	u	f
y	y	g	e	s	u	o	m	d

Answer Key * Las Respuestas

Sentences * Oraciones (page 82)

a.	3	f.	4	
b.	7	g.	5	
c.	1	h.	10	
d.	9	i.	6	
e.	2	j.	8	

Spelling Dictation * Dictado (page 82)

spine, sight, clown, reach, new, proud, place, who, cheap, snatch, fight, take, page, coin, badge; Pam threw a fast ball to the pitcher. We can eat fish and chips at the dock.

Fill in the Blank * Llene el Espacio (page 83)

1.	flour	8.	mouse	
2.	count	9.	found	
3.	mouth	10.	sound	
4.	shout	11.	Our	
5.	cloud	12.	out	
6.	south	13.	house	
7.	loud	14.	round	

Sight Words * Palabras de lectura automática (page 84)

1.	many	7.	one	
2.	some	8.	said	
3.	want	9.	There	
4.	Their	10.	been	
5.	are	11.	Could	
6.	come	12.	was	

WordSearch * Busca Palabras (page 85)

Lesson 15 * Lección 15

Word List * Lista de palabras

Las primeras doce palabras de esta lista tienen dos sílabas. Una sílaba es una parte de una palabra que se pronuncia como una unidad. Una sílaba consiste de una vocal o una vocal con una o más consonantes. Una sílaba tiene sólo un sonido vocal.

Inglés	Español
1. velvet	terciopelo
2. umpire	árbitro
3. jumbo	gigante
4. napkin	servilleta
5. tennis	tenis
6. basket	canasta
7. rabbit	conejo
8. kitten	gatito
9. problem	problema
10. absent	ausente
11. hidden	escondido
12. invite	invitar
13. sail	vela
14. sale	venta

umpire   napkin

tennis   basket

rabbit   kitten

87

Sentences * Oraciones

Lea las oraciones. Después escriba el número de la oración debajo del dibujo correcto.

1. The mouse was hidden in the pile of wood.

Dibujos

2. He had a jumbo drink with his lunch.

3. Her new dress is made of velvet.

4. The rabbit ran down the hole.

a. _____

b. _____

5. Please put the ripe plums in the basket.

6. They'll play tennis after class.

c. _____

7. Can you help me with this math problem?

d. _____

8. The small kitten will sleep in the basket.

9. The umpire called three strikes.

e. _____

10. Please put the napkin under the fork.

f. _____

g. _____

h. _____

i. _____

j. _____

Spelling Dictation * Dictado

Pídale a alguien que le dicte las palabras de la página 92. Después de escribirlas, LÉALAS y revise la ortografía. Corrija las palabras que estén equivocadas.

Fill in the Blank * Llene el Espacio

Llene cada espacio con una palabra de la lista de palabras. **Use cada palabra solamente una vez. Algunas oraciones tienen dibujos al final para ayudarle.**

1. The dog chased the _____ through the woods.

2. We will _____ Kim's friends to our house.

3. Your _____ racket is in the closet.

4. The _____ pillow is very soft.

5. The _____ called the batter out.

6. The bike has a _____ with its gears.

7. Here is a _____ of grapes for the teacher.

8. He ordered _____ fries with his meal.

9. The _____ played with the ball of string.

10. The coins were _____ in a large trunk.

11. The fishing poles are on _____ .

12. Tom was _____ from class today.

13. Please wipe your mouth with the _____ .

14. We will put up the _____ when it gets windy.

Closed Syllables * Sílabas Cerradas

Una sílaba es una parte de una palabra que se pronuncia como una unidad. Una sílaba consiste de una vocal o una vocal con una o más consonantes. Una sílaba tiene sólo un sonido vocal.

Hay seis tipos de sílabas. Un tipo de sílaba es la Sílaba Cerrada. Cuando hay dos consonantes juntas con una vocal a cada lado, la palabra se divide en sílabas entre las dos consonantes. La primera sílaba siempre es una sílaba cerrada con un sonido vocal corto.

El conocer los tipos de sílabas y la división en sílabas facilita la lectura y el deletreo. Las palabras largas pueden dividirse en sílabas y las sílabas pueden combinarse para leer o deletrear las palabras.

Lea las siguientes palabras y divídalas en sílabas. Cada palabra tiene dos sílabas cerradas. La primera ya se ha dividido.

1. velvet	vel vet	8. upset	_____
2. kitten	_____	9. album	_____
3. rabbit	_____	10. bonnet	_____
4. tennis	_____	11. combat	_____
5. hidden	_____	12. submit	_____
6. basket	_____	13. mitten	_____
7. napkin	_____	14. muffin	_____

WordSearch * Busca Palabras

Encuentra las palabras de la Lección 15 en el busca palabras. Marca las respuestas. Las palabras pueden estar escritas en forma normal, al revés o diagonalmente.

	sale	sail	jumbo
problem	absent	hidden	invite

j	q	v	n	e	d	d	i	h	s
u	u	n	a	p	k	i	n	a	i
i	o	m	d	x	e	p	i	t	m
h	d	m	b	y	y	l	a	e	e
t	n	o	e	o	a	b	w	n	t
e	e	p	y	l	s	f	u	n	i
k	t	l	x	e	b	e	s	i	v
s	t	k	n	l	a	o	l	s	n
a	i	t	f	v	e	l	r	a	i
b	k	r	a	b	b	i	t	p	s

91

Answer Key * Las Respuestas

Sentences * Oraciones (page 88)

a. 10

b. 3

c. 1

d. 5

e. 9

f. 6

g. 8

h. 4

i. 7

j. 2

Spelling Dictation * Dictado (page 88)

born, shrimp, intend, black, milk, broil, belong, rosebud, like, what, large, they, fly, broom, rainbow; Jeff plays a trombone in the band. I see smoke coming from the house.

Fill in the Blank * Llene el Espacio (page 89)

1. rabbit

2. invite

3. tennis

4. velvet

5. umpire

6. problem

7. basket

8. jumbo

9. kitten

10. hidden

11. sale

12. absent

13. napkin

14. sail

Closed Syllables * Sílabas Cerradas (page 90)

1.	vel vet	8.	up set
2.	kit ten	9.	al bum
3.	rab bit	10.	bon net
4.	ten nis	11.	com bat
5.	hid den	12.	sub mit
6.	bas ket	13.	mit ten
7.	nap kin	14.	muf fin

WordSearch * Busca Palabras (page 91)

92

Reading and Spelling Check #3
Verificación de lectura y escritura #3

Haga que alguien le dicte las siguientes palabras, leyéndolas por columnas. Escriba las palabras. Cuando haya terminado de escribirlas, léalas. Al pie de esta página, escriba tres veces las palabras que escribió mal. Busque en un diccionario todas las palabras cuyo significado no conozca.

patch	tooth	light	hardship
claw	platform	boost	grasp
boat	locker	whisper	price
point	sweeping	cupcake	lifting
beach	clear	clown	crooked

Lesson 16 * Lección 16

Word List * Lista de palabras

Las primeras doce palabras de esta lista tienen dos sílabas. Una sílaba es una parte de una palabra que se pronuncia como una unidad. Una sílaba consiste de una vocal o una vocal con una o más consonantes. Una sílaba tiene sólo un sonido vocal.

Inglés	Español
1. open	abrir
2. even	igualado
3. student	estudiante
4. zero	cero
5. bacon	tocino
6. locust	langosta
7. belong	pertenecer
8. cabin	cabaña
9. seven	siete
10. finish	terminar
11. planet	planeta
12. comet	cometa
13. pail	balde
14. pale	pálido

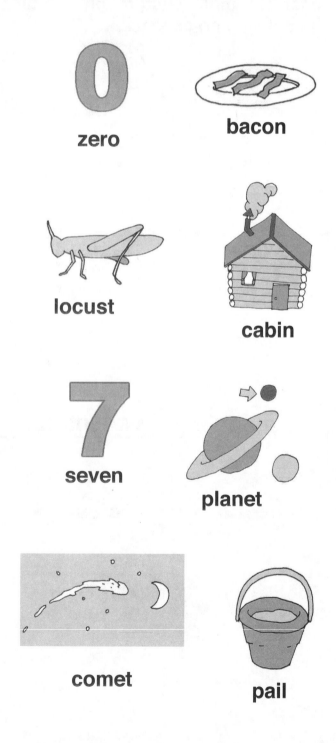

zero

bacon

locust

cabin

seven

planet

comet

pail

Sentences * Oraciones

Lea las oraciones. Después escriba el número de la oración debajo del dibujo correcto.

1. We saw a large locust in the tree.

2. The small girl can count to seven.

3. The moon is by the planet.

4. The kittens belong to the boy.

5. Please put a napkin under the bacon.

6. Today the farmer will finish painting his barn.

7. Please open the window.

8. You can put shells in your pail.

9. We found a cabin in the woods.

10. Last night we saw a comet in the sky.

Dibujos

a. _____

b. _____

c. _____

d. _____ e. _____

f. _____

g. _____

h. _____

i. _____

j. _____

Spelling Dictation * Dictado

Pídale a alguien que le dicte las palabras de la página 99. Después de escribirlas, LÉALAS y revise la ortografía. Corrija las palabras que estén equivocadas.

Fill in the Blank * Llene el Espacio

Llene cada espacio con una palabra de la lista de palabras. Use cada palabra solamente una vez. Algunas oraciones tienen dibujos al final para ayudarle.

1. Venus is a small _____ .

2. Mom will _____ her gifts now.

3. They made _____ points in the game.

4. The mice _____ in the cage.

5. The _____ is full of water.

6. He will _____ the job on Friday.

7. They own _____ horses.

8. The score was _____ at halftime.

9. The man lives in a _____ near the river.

10. The sick girl's face was _____ .

11. The _____ had a long tail.

12. The _____ studied hard for the test.

13. Mom will fry _____ for supper.

14. A _____ is an insect.

96

Open Syllables * Sílabas Abiertas

Una sílaba es una parte de una palabra que se pronuncia como una unidad. Una sílaba consiste de una vocal o una vocal con una o más consonantes. Una sílaba tiene sólo un sonido vocal.

Hay seis tipos de sílabas. Un tipo de sílaba es la Sílaba Abierta. Cuando hay una consonante entre dos vocales, la palabra puede dividirse en sílabas antes o después de la consonante sencilla. La opción de preferencia es tratar de dividir antes de la consonante. La primera sílaba será abierta y la vocal será larga. Cuando haya una vocal corta en la primera sílaba, interrumpa después de la consonante y la primera sílaba será cerrada.

El conocer los tipos de sílabas y la división en sílabas facilita la lectura y el deletreo. Las palabras largas pueden dividirse en sílabas y las sílabas pueden combinarse para leer o deletrear las palabras.

Lea las siguientes palabras y divídalas en sílabas. Cada palabra tiene dos sílabas. Las primeras sílabas de ciertas palabras serán abiertas y otras palabras tendrán primeras sílabas cerradas. Las primeras dos ya se han dividido.

1. open	o pen	8. locust	
2. comet	com et	9. finish	
3. even		10. seven	
4. student		11. belong	
5. planet		12. cabin	
6. bacon		13. robin	
7. zero		14. rapid	

WordSearch * Busca Palabras

Encuentra las palabras de la Lección 16 en el busca palabras. Marca las respuestas. Las palabras pueden estar escritas en forma normal, al revés o diagonalmente.

	0		
		finish	**open**
even	**student**	**belong**	**pale**

e	l	o	c	u	s	t	o	t
b	v	z	e	r	o	p	p	p
h	c	e	l	a	e	s	a	b
s	a	g	n	n	t	l	t	a
i	b	o	n	u	e	f	o	c
n	i	w	d	o	l	v	b	o
i	n	e	k	d	l	i	n	n
f	n	i	n	g	d	e	a	q
t	t	e	n	a	l	p	b	p

Answer Key * Las Respuestas

Sentences * Oraciones (page 95)

a.	3	f.	5
b.	6	g.	4
c.	1	h.	2
d.	7	i.	10
e.	9	j.	8

Spelling Dictation * Dictado (page 95)

pork, hand, when, compact, clock, melt, looking, painter, point, polo, airplane, grow, pine, done, card; I want to see your new house. Tom was absent from the game.

Fill in the Blank * Llene el Espacio (page 96)

1.	planet		8.	even
2.	open		9.	cabin
3.	zero		10.	pale
4.	belong		11.	comet
5.	pail		12.	student
6.	finish		13.	bacon
7.	seven		14.	locust

Open Syllables * Sílabas Abiertas (page 97)

1. o pen	8. lo cust
2. com et	9. fin ish
3. e ven	10. sev en
4. stu dent	11. be long
5. plan et	12. cab in
6. ba con	13. rob in
7. ze ro	14. rap id

WordSearch * Busca Palabras (page 98)

Lesson 17 * Lección 17

Word List * Lista de palabras

Las primeras doce palabras de esta lista tienen dos sílabas. Una sílaba es una parte de una palabra que se pronuncia como una unidad. Una sílaba consiste de una vocal o una vocal con una o más consonantes. Una sílaba tiene sólo un sonido vocal.

Inglés	Español
1. sandwich	sándwich
2. monster	monstruo
3. pumpkin	calabaza
4. dandruff	caspa
5. empress	emperatriz
6. impress	causar buena impresión
7. kingdom	reino
8. emblem	emblema
9. hundred	cien
10. upgrade	mejorar
11. inspire	inspirar
12. complex	complejo
13. bear	oso
14. bare	pocos muebles

sandwich

monster

pumpkin

empress

emblem

100

hundred

bear

Sentences * Oraciones

Lea las oraciones. Después escriba el número de la oración debajo del dibujo correcto.

1. She will impress her mom with good grades.

    Dibujos

2. The brown bear has long sharp claws.

3. He has a sport's emblem on his jacket.

8. His kingdom has many flowers.

    a. _____

    b. _____

5. She will carve a face on the pumpkin.

6. The empress wore a long green dress.

    c. _____

7. He thinks there is a monster in the closet.

8. That man is one hundred years old.

    e. _____

9. I will finish the sandwich later.

    d. _____

10. That math problem is very complex.

    f. _____

g. _____   h. _____   i. _____

j. _____

Spelling Dictation * Dictado

Pídale a alguien que le dicte las palabras de la página 105. Después de escribirlas, LÉALAS y revise la ortografía. Corrija las palabras que estén equivocadas.

Fill in the Blank * Llene el Espacio

Llene cada espacio con una palabra de la lista de palabras. Use cada palabra solamente una vez. Algunas oraciones tienen dibujos al final para ayudarle.

1. He has three _____ books.   **100**

2. He will _____ his friend with his new car.

3. The _____ stood on its hind legs.

4. The truck's gears are very _____ .

5. We will make _____ pie for dinner.

6. She will _____ her ticket to first class.

7. The team's _____ is a large bear.

8. I will brush the _____ off my dark dress.

9. The _____ ate a sandwich for lunch.

10. The coach will _____ the team to do well.

11. On the paper, she drew a large _____ .

12. Inside, the cabin was _____ .

13. She had a ham _____ for a snack.

14. The king and queen have a large _____ .

Syllables * Sílabas

Una sílaba es una parte de una palabra que se pronuncia como una unidad. Una sílaba consiste de una vocal o una vocal con una o más consonantes. Una sílaba tiene sólo un sonido vocal.

El conocer los tipos de sílabas y la división en sílabas facilita la lectura y el deletreo. Las palabras largas pueden dividirse en sílabas y las sílabas pueden combinarse para leer o deletrear las palabras.

Cuando hay tres consonantes entre dos vocales, la sílaba puede dividirse antes o después de la consonante media. Las dos consonantes que permanecen juntas son por lo general una mezcla común o dígrafo.

Lea las siguientes palabras y divídalas en sílabas. Cada palabra tiene dos sílabas. La primera ya se ha dividido.

1. sandwich	sand wich	11. emblem	
2. monster		12. hundred	
3. pumpkin		13. upgrade	
4. dandruff		14. inspire	
5. empress		15. complex	
6. impress		16. transmit	
7. kingdom		17. inspect	
8. contrast		18. imprint	
9. fondness		19. dangling	
10. humdrum		20. frankness	

WordSearch * Busca Palabras

Encuentra las palabras de la Lección 17 en el busca palabras. Marca las respuestas. Las palabras pueden estar escritas en forma normal, al revés o diagonalmente.

100			
	dandruff	impress	kingdom
inspire	complex	bare	

r	v	d	d	e	r	d	n	u	h	b
o	e	r	e	m	b	l	e	m	a	d
v	t	k	a	h	c	w	g	r	d	w
a	q	i	s	e	a	n	e	a	h	s
x	s	n	j	a	b	h	n	i	h	s
e	s	g	s	o	n	d	z	o	g	e
l	e	d	m	y	r	d	f	e	m	r
p	r	o	g	u	y	d	w	s	v	p
m	p	m	f	q	j	m	g	i	n	m
o	m	f	s	g	e	h	l	b	c	i
c	e	b	e	r	i	p	s	n	i	h

Answer Key * Las Respuestas

Sentences * Oraciones (page 101)

a. 8

b. 5

c. 4

d. 1

e. 7

f. 9

g. 2

h. 6

i. 3

j. 10

Spelling Dictation * Dictado (page 101)

torn, act, stuck, window, invite, cart, does, pool, mend, radish, squall, quack, open, join, drift; Sam marched with the small band. It is cool under the tree.

Fill in the Blank * Llene el Espacio (page 102)

1. hundred
2. impress
3. bear
4. complex
5. pumpkin
6. upgrade
7. emblem

8. dandruff
9. empress
10. inspire
11. monster
12. bare
13. sandwich
14. kingdom

Syllables * Sílabas (page 103)

1.	sand	wich	11.	em blem
2.	mon	ster	12.	hun dred
3.	pump	kin	13.	up grade
4.	dan	druff	14.	in spire
5.	em	press	15.	com plex
6.	im	press	16.	trans mit
7.	king	dom	17.	in spect
8.	con	trast	18.	im print
9.	fond	ness	19.	dan gling
10.	hum	drum	20.	frank ness

WordSearch * Busca Palabras (page 104)

Lesson 18 * Lección 18

Word List * Lista de palabras

Las primeras doce palabras de esta lista tienen dos sílabas. Una sílaba es una parte de una palabra que se pronuncia como una unidad. Una sílaba consiste de una vocal o una vocal con una o más consonantes. Una sílaba tiene sólo un sonido vocal.

Inglés	Español
1. dislike	desagradar
2. mistake	equivocación
3. empire	imperio
4. bonfire	fogata
5. complete	completar
6. ignore	ignorar
7. escape	escapar
8. include	incluir
9. entire	entero
10. athlete	atleta
11. tadpole	renacuajo
12. trombone	trombón
13. hair	pelo
14. hare	liebre

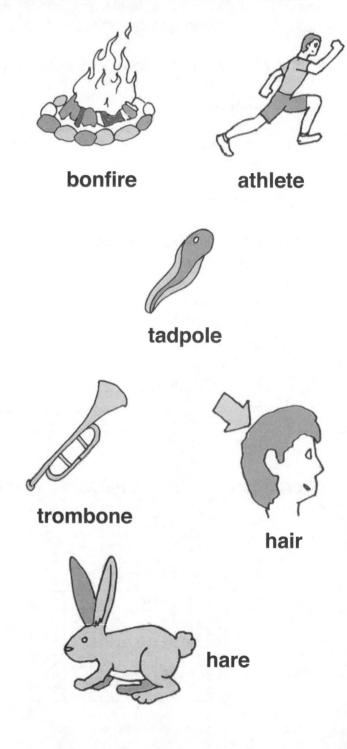

bonfire   athlete

tadpole

trombone

hair

hare

Sentences * Oraciones

Lea las oraciones. Después escriba el número de la oración debajo del dibujo correcto.

1. They will roast marshmallows at the bonfire. **Dibujos**

2. The tadpole will become a frog.

3. She is a very good athlete.

a. _____

9. Two pencils were included with the book.

b. _____

5. The prisoner escaped from jail.

6. The kitten ignored the bacon.

c. _____

7. The small boy ate the entire pie.

8. The girl's hair is down to her waist.

9. We saw a large hare in the desert.

d. _____

e. _____

10. She plays the trombone in the marching band.

f. _____

g. _____

h. _____

i. _____

j. _____

Spelling Dictation * Dictado

Pídale a alguien que le dicte las palabras de la página 111. Después de escribirlas, LÉALAS y revise la ortografía. Corrija las palabras que estén equivocadas.

Fill in the Blank * Llene el Espacio

Llene cada espacio con una palabra de la lista de palabras. Use cada palabra solamente una vez. Algunas oraciones tienen dibujos al final para ayudarle.

1. The _____ makes a loud sound.

2. They _____ bacon in their sandwiches.

3. The _____ exercises every day.

4. It was a _____ to invite five boys to our house.

5. We will _____ a free basket with the kitten.

6. She will _____ one hundred math problems.

7. The river was the northern border of the _____ .

8. The _____ has two hind legs.

9. Jack spent the _____ year in Spain.

10. Your _____ is too short for braids.

11. We will _____ the loud sound.

12. Who will bring wood for the _____ ?

13. Don't let the puppy _____ from the yard.

14. The _____ hopped into the cave.

Syllables * Sílabas

Una sílaba es una parte de una palabra que se pronuncia como una unidad. Una sílaba consiste de una vocal o una vocal con una o más consonantes. Una sílaba tiene sólo un sonido vocal.

Hay seis tipos de sílabas. Una sílaba abierta tiene un sonido vocal largo al final de la sílaba. Por ejemplo: me, be, my. Una sílaba cerrada tiene un sonido vocal corto seguido de una o más consonantes. Ejemplo: bug, hill, math. Las sílabas de <u>e</u> muda tienen una <u>e</u> muda al final de la sílaba, lo cual alarga la vocal precedente. Ejemplo: dime, sale, bake. Éstos son tres tipos de sílabas.

Open/Abierta	Closed/Cerrada	Silent E/E muda
so	hop	like
ti	cup	vite
sta	rab	pire

Lea y marque los diferentes tipos de sílabas. La primera ya se ha marcado.

O = Open, C = Closed, E = Silent E

1. <u>C</u> bas	6. ___ vel	11. ___ me	16. ___ ale
2. ___ oll	7. ___ dime	12. ___ jum	17. ___ nis
3. ___ cu	8. ___ kit	13. ___ vite	18. ___ bo
4. ___ stum	9. ___ go	14. ___ ab	19. ___ prob
5. ___ spo	10. ___ ame	15. ___ um	20. ___ up

WordSearch * Busca Palabras

Encuentra las palabras de la Lección 18 en el busca palabras. Marca las respuestas. Las palabras pueden estar escritas en forma normal, al revés o diagonalmente.

	dislike	**mistake**	**complete**
include	**entire**		

h	g	e	r	i	f	n	o	b	e
e	a	c	d	m	z	t	t	r	e
d	v	i	o	r	b	r	a	n	k
u	j	j	r	m	o	h	q	b	a
l	r	w	l	m	p	r	j	u	t
c	o	b	b	t	t	l	k	y	s
n	j	o	j	n	l	c	e	j	i
i	n	e	r	i	t	n	e	t	m
e	d	i	s	l	i	k	e	h	e
g	g	y	e	t	e	l	h	t	a

Answer Key * Las Respuestas

Sentences * Oraciones (page 107)

a.	4	f.	9
b.	7	g.	8
c.	2	h.	1
d.	6	i.	10
e.	5	j.	3

Spelling Dictation * Dicatado (page 107)

park, thick, blow, her, would, sunshine, there, cry, boil, goes, reptile, pool, storm, inflate, down; The bank clerk will give us cash. We found the box while you were gone.

Fill in the Blank * Llene el Espacio (page 108)

1. trombone
2. dislike
3. athlete
4. mistake
5. include
6. complete
7. empire
8. tadpole
9. entire
10. hair
11. ignore
12. bonfire
13. escape
14. hare

Syllables * Sílabas (page 109)

1. C	6. C	11. O	16. E
2. C	7. E	12. C	17. C
3. O	8. C	13. E	18. O
4. C	9. O	14. C	19. C
5. O	10. E	15. C	20. C

WordSearch * Busca Palabras (page 110)

Lesson 19 * Lección 19

Word List * Lista de palabras

Las primeras doce palabras de esta lista tienen dos sílabas. Una sílaba es una parte de una palabra que se pronuncia como una unidad. Una sílaba consiste de una vocal o una vocal con una o más consonantes. Una sílaba tiene sólo un sonido vocal.

Inglés	Español
1. cartoon	dibujos animados
2. marker	marcador
3. boxer	boxeador
4. carton	cartón
5. player	jugador
6. farther	más lejos
7. smarter	más listo
8. locker	armario
9. smoother	más uniforme
10. carpet	alfombra
11. hanger	percha
12. former	antiguo
13. pear	pera
14. pair	par

marker

boxer

carton

locker

hanger

pear

Sentences * Oraciones

Lea las oraciones. Después escriba el número de la oración debajo del dibujo correcto.

1. Please buy a carton of milk at the store.

Dibujos

2. We will put our clothes in the locker.

3. The red marker is in the basket.

4. She picked a ripe pear for lunch.

a. _____

b. _____

5. Meg threw the ball farther than Jan.

6. Please roll up the carpet.

7. The basketball player is very tall.

c. _____

8. Which boxer won the fight last night?

d. _____

9. Pat will wear the red pair of shorts.

e. _____

10. He likes to watch cartoons in the morning.

f. _____

g. _____

h. _____

i. _____

j. _____

Spelling Dictation * Dicatado

Pídale a alguien que le dicte las palabras de la página 117. Después de escribirlas, LÉALAS y revise la ortografía. Corrija las palabras que estén equivocadas.

Fill in the Blank * Llene el Espacio

Llene cada espacio con una palabra de la lista de palabras. Use cada palabra solamente una vez. Algunas oraciones tienen dibujos al final para ayudarle.

1. Would you like a _____ for a snack?

2. The black dog is _____ than the brown dog.

3. I will buy one _____ of eggs.

4. Which _____ do you want to watch?

5. The _____ wore blue shorts with red stripes.

6. She will buy a _____ of mittens for the trip.

7. Our _____ is down this hall.

8. There is an oil spot on the new _____ .

9. This road is _____ than the other one.

10. _____ number ten is my sister's friend.

11. There is a silk _____ in the bedroom closet.

12. Yesterday the track team ran _____ .

13. Use a _____ to write your name on the ball.

14. The coach is a _____ football player.

Syllable Division * División en sílabas

Una sílaba es una parte de una palabra que se pronuncia como una unidad. Una sílaba consiste de una vocal o una vocal con una o más consonantes. Una sílaba tiene sólo un sonido vocal.

Hay seis tipos de sílabas. Una sílaba abierta tiene un sonido vocal largo al final de la sílaba. Por ejemplo: me, be, my. Una sílaba cerrada tiene un sonido vocal corto seguido de una o más consonantes. Ejemplo: bug, hill, math. Las sílabas de e muda tienen una e muda al final de la sílaba, lo cual alarga la vocal precedente. Ejemplo: dime, sale, bake. Una sílaba controlada por una r contiene una vocal seguida de una r. Ejemplos: card, form, her. Éstos son cuatro tipos de sílabas.

Open/Abierta	Closed/Cerrada	Silent E/E muda	R Controlled Controlada por R
so	hop	like	ter
ti	cup	vite	car
sta	rab	pire	cor

Lea las palabras. Divida cada palabra en sílabas. Luego marque los tipos de sílabas. La primera ya se ha marcado.

O = Open, C = Closed, E = Silent E, R = R Controlled

1. buzzer	C R buzz er	9. boxer	_____
2. carton	_____	10. hero	_____
3. marker	_____	11. eject	_____
4. farther	_____	12. menu	_____
5. smarter	_____	13. erase	_____
6. locker	_____	14. vanish	_____
7. carpet	_____	15. relish	_____
8. hanger	_____	16. inflate	_____

WordSearch * Busca Palabras

Encuentra las palabras de la Lección 19 en el busca palabras. Marca las respuestas. Las palabras pueden estar escritas en forma normal, al revés o diagonalmente.

cartoon	farther	smarter	smoother
carpet	former	pair	

f	r	a	x	h	r	n	r	r	c
o	h	e	s	c	o	u	j	e	a
r	v	r	h	o	g	q	j	g	r
m	t	s	t	t	p	n	t	n	p
e	t	r	p	o	o	e	g	a	e
r	a	a	h	c	o	o	a	h	t
c	i	r	e	x	o	b	m	r	n
r	c	a	r	t	o	n	b	s	y
f	a	r	t	h	e	r	p	x	s
o	i	n	r	e	t	r	a	m	s

Answer Key * Las Respuestas

Sentences * Oraciones (page 113)

a. 5
b. 4
c. 1
d. 2
e. 6

f. 7
g. 8
h. 3
i. 9
j. 10

Spelling Dictation * Dictado (page 113)

should, dodge, whisper, fern, mowing, napkin, problem, stitch, lace, jumbo, huge, shadow, lender, race, power; May is twisting the top off the jar. The tall man is standing on the runway.

Fill in the Blank * Llene el Espacio (page 114)

1. pear
2. smarter
3. carton
4. cartoon
5. boxer
6. pair
7. locker

8. carpet
9. smoother
10. Player
11. hanger
12. farther
13. marker
14. former

Syllable Division * División en sílabas (page 115)

	C R		R R		C R		O E
1.	buzz er	5.	smar ter	9.	box er	13.	e rase
	R C		C R		O O		C C
2.	car ton	6.	lock er	10.	he ro	14.	van ish
	R R		R C		O C		C C
3.	mar ker	7.	car pet	11.	e ject	15.	rel ish
	R R		C R		C O		C E
4.	far ther	8.	hang er	12.	men u	16.	in flate

WordSearch * Busca Palabras (page 116)

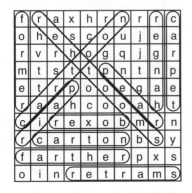

117

Lesson 20 * Lección 20

Word List * Lista de palabras

Las primeras doce palabras tienen dos sílabas. Una sílaba es de un par de vocales. Una sílaba de un par de vocales tiene dos vocales juntas que forman un sonido. Cuando y y w se combinan con una vocal para formar un sonido vocal, a la y y a la w también se les llama vocales.

Inglés	Español
1. boiling	hirviendo
2. canteen	cantimplora
3. sleeping	durmiendo
4. drooping	ponerse mustio
5. tower	torre
6. power	electricidad
7. shower	ducha
8. soybean	soja
9. maybe	quizá
10. lower	bajar
11. rowing	remar
12. sorting	clasificar
13. sea	mar
14. see	ver

canteen

sleeping

drooping

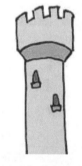

tower

shower

soybean

Sentences * Oraciones

Lea las oraciones. Después escriba el número de la oración debajo del dibujo correcto.

1. The water is boiling in the large pot.

2. The flower is drooping in the hot sun.

3. He is rowing across the lake.

4. The boys are sleeping under the tree.

5. Every morning I take a hot shower.

6. He is sorting his coins into piles.

7. Dan is standing at the top of the tower.

8. I can see the sea from here.

9. Fill the canteen with cold water.

10. The small girl will sleep on the lower bunk.

Dibujos

a. _____

b. _____

c. _____

d. _____

e. _____

f. _____

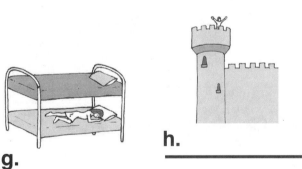

g. _____

h. _____

i. _____

j. _____

Spelling Dictation * Dictado

Pídale a alguien que le dicte las palabras de la página 123. Después de escribirlas, LÉALAS y revise la ortografía. Corrija las palabras que estén equivocadas.

Fill in the Blank * Llene el Espacio

Llene cada espacio con una palabra de la lista de palabras. Use cada palabra solamente una vez. Algunas oraciones tienen dibujos al final para ayudarle.

1. The girl made a tall _____ with the blocks.

2. The _____ was as smooth as glass.

3. He took a large _____ on the hike.

4. The large ship will _____ the lifeboats.

5. The monster is _____ in the closet.

6. The _____ was out for five days.

7. The dog did not eat the _____ .

8. _____ we can visit the White House.

9. He will put the lobster in the _____ water.

10. Sam likes to sing in the _____ .

11. Peg is _____ her boat in the rain.

12. I can _____ the mouse in the corner.

13. The _____ flowers need water.

14. The boy is _____ his toys by size.

Syllable Division * División en sílabas

El conocer los tipos de sílabas y la división en sílabas facilita la lectura y el deletreo. Las palabras largas pueden dividirse en sílabas y las sílabas pueden combinarse para leer o deletrear las palabras. Hay seis tipos de sílabas. La siguiente tabla muestra cinco tipos.

Open/Abierta	Closed/Cerrada	Silent E E muda	R Controlled Controlada por R	Vowel Pair Par de vocales
so	hop	like	ter	may
ti	cup	vite	car	now
sta	rab	pire	cor	fee

Lea las palabras. Divida cada palabra en sílabas. Luego marque los tipos de sílabas. La primera ya se ha marcado.

O = Open, C = Closed, E = Silent E, R = R controlled, VP = Vowel Pair

	O C wo ven		
1. woven		13. sorting	
2. boiling		14. shifting	
3. canteen		15. flavor	
4. sleeping		16. level	
5. drooping		17. fiber	
6. tower		18. comet	
7. power		19. porter	
8. shower		20. cooler	
9. soybean		21. window	
10. maybe		22. sooner	
11. lower		23. vacant	
12. rowing		24. tiger	

WordSearch * Busca Palabras

Encuentra las palabras de la Lección 20 en el busca palabras. Marca las respuestas. Las palabras pueden estar escritas en forma normal, al revés o diagonalmente.

	boiling	**power**	**maybe**
lower	**rowing**	**sorting**	**sea**
see			

c	a	n	t	e	e	n	z	d	s
e	e	g	v	d	j	y	r	a	o
g	r	e	n	g	f	o	e	t	y
n	e	n	s	i	o	s	i	o	b
i	w	s	c	p	p	f	i	w	e
l	o	i	i	r	m	e	l	e	a
i	p	n	e	d	q	a	e	r	n
o	g	w	b	x	y	j	y	l	s
b	o	g	n	i	w	o	r	b	s
l	r	g	n	i	t	r	o	s	e

Answer Key * Las Respuestas

Sentences * Oraciones (page 119)

a.	9	f.	8
b.	6	g.	10
c.	3	h.	7
d.	2	i.	5
e.	1	j.	4

Spelling Dictation * Dictado (page 119)

some, wanting, hamster, blinker, fry, picking, could, crutch, hedge, mall, crafts, when, locate, spoiling, very; She can see the deer from her window. They were stacking logs by the fence.

Fill in the Blank * Llene el Espacio (page 120)

1. tower
2. sea
3. canteen
4. lower
5. sleeping
6. power
7. soybean
8. Maybe
9. boiling
10. shower
11. rowing
12. see
13. drooping
14. sorting

Syllable Division * División en sílabas (page 121)

1. wo (O) ven (C)	7. pow (VP) er (R)	13. sort (R) ing (C)	19. por (R) ter (R)
2. boil (VP) ing (C)	8. show (VP) er (R)	14. shift (C) ing (C)	20. cool (VP) er (R)
3. can (C) teen (VP)	9. soy (VP) bean (VP)	15. fla (O) vor (R)	21. win (C) dow (VP)
4. sleep (VP) ing (C)	10. may (VP) be (O)	16. lev (C) el (C)	22. soon (VP) er (R)
5. droop (VP) ing (C)	11. low (VP) er (R)	17. fi (O) ber (R)	23. va (O) cant (C)
6. tow (VP) er (R)	12. row (VP) ing (C)	18. com (C) et (C)	24. ti (O) ger (R)

WordSearch * Busca Palabras (page 122)

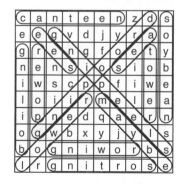

123

Reading and Spelling Check #4
Verificación de lectura y escritura #4

Haga que alguien le dicte las siguientes palabras, leyéndolas por columnas. Escriba las palabras. Cuando haya terminado de escribirlas, léalas. Al pie de esta página, escriba tres veces las palabras que escribió mal. Busque en un diccionario todas las palabras cuyo significado no conozca.

match	frown	charm	napkin
center	lodge	flower	blowing
done	smoother	joint	fringe
sorting	could	crow	space
clump	germ	very	clerk

English Translation of Spanish Directions

Lesson 1

Page 1: A suffix is added to the end of a root or base word. For example with *calling*: <u>call</u> is the base word and <u>ing</u> is the suffix.

Page 2: Read the sentences. Then put the number of the sentence under the correct picture. **Spelling Dictation** Have someone dictate the words on page 6 to you. After you have written the words READ THE WORDS and check to make sure they are spelled correctly. Correct any words that are misspelled.

Page 3: Fill in each blank with a word from the Word List. Use each word once. Some sentences have pictures at the end to help you.

Page 4: The suffix <u>ing</u> is a vowel suffix because it starts with a vowel. When a vowel suffix is added to a word ending with a vowel, the ending vowel on the base word is dropped before the vowel suffix is added. Example: *make* becomes *making*. **Add** the vowel suffix <u>ing</u> to the following verbs. (Remember a verb is an action word.) When the suffix <u>ing</u> is added to the end of a verb, it means the action is happening now. **Use** the verbs from above to fill in the blanks. Use each verb once.

Page 5: Find the words from Lesson 1 in the WordSearch. Circle the words. The words can be written across, in reverse, or diagonal.

Lesson 2

Page 7: The sound /er/ as in *her* is found in the middle or at the end of a word. Often at the end of a word the /er/ sound is a suffix.

Page 8: Read the sentences. Then put the number of the sentence under the correct picture. **Spelling Dictation** Have someone dictate the words on page 12 to you. After you have written the words READ THE WORDS and check to make sure they are spelled correctly. Correct any words that are misspelled.

Page 9: Fill in each blank with a word from the Word List. Use each word once. Some sentences have pictures at the end to help you.

Page 10: A suffix is added after a root or base word. The suffix <u>ed</u> is a vowel suffix because it starts with a vowel. When a vowel suffix is added to a word ending with a vowel, the ending vowel on the base word is dropped before the vowel suffix is added. Example: *bake* becomes *baked.* **Add** the vowel suffix <u>ed</u> to the following verbs. (Remember a verb is an action word.) When <u>ed</u> is added to the end of verb, it means the action has already happened. The suffix <u>ed</u> is spoken phonetically in three different ways: /d/, /t/, and /ed/. **Use** the verbs from above to fill in the blanks. Use each verb once.

Page 11: Find the words from Lesson 2 in the WordSearch. Circle the words. The words can be written across, in reverse, or diagonal.

Lesson 3

Page 13: The letters –tch make the /ch/ sound as in *match*. Rule: -tch is used after a short vowel and usually at the end of a word. Otherwise the /ch/ sound is spelled ch when it follows a consonant or a vowel team as in *ranch, speech*, and *porch*. The last four words in this list are exceptions to the rule.

Page 14: Read the sentences. Then put the number of the sentence under the correct picture. **Spelling Dictation** Have someone dictate the words on page 18 to you. After you have written the words READ THE WORDS and check to make sure they are spelled correctly. Correct any words that are misspelled.

Page 15: Fill in each blank with a word from the Word List. Use each word once. Some sentences have pictures at the end to help you.

Page 16: Add es to words that end in s, x, z, ch, or sh. Otherwise add an s. **Use** the words from above to fill in the blanks. Use each verb once.

Page 17: Find the words from Lesson 3 in the WordSearch. Circle the words. The words can be written across, in reverse, or diagonal.

Lesson 4

Page 19: The letters –dge make the /j/ sound as in *badge*. Rule: -dge is used after a short vowel and usually at the end of a word. Otherwise the /j/ sound is spell -ge when it follows a consonant, vowel pair, or a long vowel as in *fringe, barge, page*.

Page 20: Read the sentences. Then put the number of the sentence under the correct picture. **Spelling Dictation** Have someone dictate the words on page 24 to you. After you have written the words READ THE WORDS and check to make sure they are spelled correctly. Correct any words that are misspelled.

Page 21: Fill in each blank with a word from the Word List. Use each word once. Some sentences have pictures at the end to help you.

Page 22: The vowel e is the most often used letter in the English language. Some letters in English are never used in the final position in a word such as j and v. Therefore we have the spelling –dge and –ge for /j/ as in *lodge* and *page*. Words ending with the /v/ sound have the silent marker e at the end of the word. Use the following words in the sentences below. **The** silent marker e also keeps some words from looking like plurals. Use the following words in the sentences below.

Page 23: Find the words from Lesson 4 in the WordSearch. Circle the words. The words can be written across, in reverse, or diagonal.

Lesson 5

Page 25: The letters <u>aw</u> say /aw/ as in *jaw*. Rule: <u>aw</u> is usually at the end of a word or followed by <u>n</u> or <u>l</u>.

Page 26: Read the sentences. Then put the number of the sentence under the correct picture. **Spelling Dictation** Have someone dictate the words on page 30 to you. After you have written the words READ THE WORDS and check to make sure they are spelled correctly. Correct any words that are misspelled.

Page 27: Fill in each blank with a word from the Word List. Use each word once. Some sentences have pictures at the end to help you.

Page 28: Compound Words combine two small words to make one word. Write the two small words that make up the one large word. **Fill** in the blanks with one of the compound words.

Page 29: Find the words from Lesson 5 in the WordSearch. Circle the words. The words can be written across, in reverse, or diagonal.

Reading and Spelling Check #1

Page 31: Have someone dictate the following words to you, reading down the columns. Write the words. When you have finished writing the words, read the words. At the bottom of this page, write any misspelled words three times. Look up the words in a dictionary if you do not know their meanings.

Lesson 6

Page 32: The letters <u>oa</u> say long /o/ as in *boat*. Rule: <u>oa</u> makes the long <u>o</u> sound and comes at the beginning or middle of short words.

Page 33: Read the sentences. Then put the number of the sentence under the correct picture. **Spelling Dictation** Have someone dictate the words on page 37 to you. After you have written the words READ THE WORDS and check to make sure they are spelled correctly. Correct any words that are misspelled.

Page 34: Fill in each blank with a word from the Word List. Use each word once. Some sentences have pictures at the end to help you.

Page 35: In one-syllable words with one short vowel followed by one consonant, the final consonant needs to be doubled before adding a vowel suffix (an ending that begins with a vowel). **Fill** in the table with the correct spelling for each word. The letter <u>y</u> is often used as a vowel. The above rule applies when adding a <u>y</u> suffix. Fill in the table with the correct word.

Page 36: Find the words from Lesson 6 in the WordSearch. Circle the words. The words can be written across, in reverse, or diagonal.

Lesson 7

Page 38: The letters <u>oi</u> say /oi/ as in *boil*. Rule: <u>oi</u> comes at the beginning or in the middle of a word. The letters <u>oy</u> make the same sound but come at the end of a word.

Page 39: Read the sentences. Then put the number of the sentence under the correct picture. **Spelling Dictation** Have someone dictate the words on page 43 to you. After you have written the words READ THE WORDS and check to make sure they are spelled correctly. Correct any words that are misspelled.

Page 40: Fill in each blank with a word from the Word List. Use each word once. Some sentences have pictures at the end to help you.

Page 41: When adding <u>s</u> to words that end in <u>y</u>, you must change the <u>y</u> to <u>i</u> and then add <u>es</u> if the <u>y</u> is preceded by a consonant. If the <u>y</u> is preceded by a vowel, just add <u>s</u>. The pronunciation of the <u>s</u> either way will be the /z/ sound. **Fill** in the blanks with the words below. Add <u>s</u> to each word, following the rules above.

Page 42: Find the words from Lesson 7 in the WordSearch. Circle the words. The words can be written across, in reverse, or diagonal.

Lesson 8

Page 44: In this list, the letter <u>c</u> says /s/ as in *nice*. Rule: The letter <u>c</u> makes the /s/ sound when it is followed by an <u>e</u>, <u>i</u>, or <u>y</u>.

Page 45: Read the sentences. Then put the number of the sentence under the correct picture. **Spelling Dictation** Have someone dictate the words on page 49 to you. After you have written the words READ THE WORDS and check to make sure they are spelled correctly. Correct any words that are misspelled.

Page 46: Fill in each blank with a word from the Word List. Use each word once. Some sentences have pictures at the end to help you.

Page 47: In each sentence the underlined word is either a noun or a verb. A noun names a person, creature, place or thing. A verb is an action word. After each sentence write *verb* or *noun* depending on how the underlined word is used. The first one has been done for you.

Page 48: Find the words from Lesson 8 in the WordSearch. Circle the words. The words can be written across, in reverse, or diagonal.

Lesson 9

Page 50: In this list, the letter g says /j/ as in *page*. Rule: The letter g makes the /j/ sound when it is followed by an e, i, or y.

Page 51: Read the sentences. Then put the number of the sentence under the correct picture. **Spelling Dictation** Have someone dictate the words on page 55 to you. After you have written the words READ THE WORDS and check to make sure they are spelled correctly. Correct any words that are misspelled.

Page 52: Fill in each blank with a word from the Word List. Use each word once. Some sentences have pictures at the end to help you.

Page 53: In each sentence the underlined word is either a noun or a verb. A noun names a person, creature, place or thing. A verb is an action word. After each sentence write *verb* or *noun* depending on how the underlined word is used. The first one has been done for you.

Page 54: Find the words from Lesson 9 in the WordSearch. Circle the words. The words can be written across, in reverse, or diagonal.

Lesson 10

Page 56: The letters ea sound like long /e/ as in *eat*. The letters ea are a vowel team. Often the first vowel in a vowel team will say its name and the second vowel is silent. There is no sound difference between ea and ee.

Page 57: Read the sentences. Then put the number of the sentence under the correct picture. **Spelling Dictation** Have someone dictate the words on page 61 to you. After you have written the words READ THE WORDS and check to make sure they are spelled correctly. Correct any words that are misspelled.

Page 58: Fill in each blank with a word from the Word List. Use each word once. Some sentences have pictures at the end to help you.

Page 59: In Spanish there are only two contractions: *del* (de + el) and *al* (al + el). In English they are very common. Join two words and take away one or two letters. Put an apostrophe where you omit the letters. **Write** a sentence with each contraction from the table.

Page 60: Find the words from Lesson 10 in the WordSearch. Circle the words. The words can be written across, in reverse, or diagonal.

Reading and Spelling Check #2

Page 62: Have someone dictate the following words to you, reading down the columns. Write the words. When you have finished writing the words, read the words. At the bottom of this page, write any misspelled words three times. Look up the words in a dictionary if you do not know their meanings.

Lesson 11

Page 63: The letters ew say /oo/ as in *new*. The spelling ew is the first choice for writing the /oo/ sound at the end of a word.

Page 64: Read the sentences. Then put the number of the sentence under the correct picture. **Spelling Dictation** Have someone dictate the words on page 68 to you. After you have written the words READ THE WORDS and check to make sure they are spelled correctly. Correct any words that are misspelled.

Page 65: Fill in each blank with a word from the Word List. Use each word once. Some sentences have pictures at the end to help you.

Page 66: In Spanish there are only two contractions: *del* (de + el) and *al* (al + el). In English they are very common. Join two words and take away one or two letters. Put an apostrophe where you omit the letters. **Write** a sentence with each contraction from the table.

Page 67: Find the words from Lesson 11 in the WordSearch. Circle the words. The words can be written across, in reverse, or diagonal.

Lesson 12

Page 69: In this list, ear says /ear/ as in *hear*.

Page 70: Read the sentences. Then put the number of the sentence under the correct picture. **Spelling Dictation** Have someone dictate the words on page 74 to you. After you have written the words READ THE WORDS and check to make sure they are spelled correctly. Correct any words that are misspelled.

Page 71: Fill in each blank with a word from the Word List. Use each word once. Some sentences have pictures at the end to help you.

Page 72: A base word is the word before any affixes are added. Write the base word of each word below. The first one has been done for you. **Sight** words are common words that often do not follow the rules. These words need to be spelled correctly because they are used often.

Page 73: Find the words from Lesson 12 in the WordSearch. Circle the words. The words can be written across, in reverse, or diagonal.

Lesson 13

Page 75: The letters igh say the long /i/ sound as in *night*. The letters igh are usually at the end of a word or followed by the letter t.

Page 76: Read the sentences. Then put the number of the sentence under the correct picture. **Spelling Dictation** Have someone dictate the words on page 80 to you. After you have written the words READ THE WORDS and check to make sure they are spelled correctly. Correct any words that are misspelled.

Page 77: Fill in each blank with a word from the Word List. Use each word once. Some sentences have pictures at the end to help you.

Page 78: The following are common words that do not follow the spelling rules. **Use** each sight word once to fill in the blanks.

Page 79: Find the words from Lesson 13 in the WordSearch. Circle the words. The words can be written across, in reverse, or diagonal.

Lesson 14

Page 81: The letters ou say /ou/ as in house. Rule: ou is the first choice for this sound in the middle of a word.

Page 82: Read the sentences. Then put the number of the sentence under the correct picture. **Spelling Dictation** Have someone dictate the words on page 86 to you. After you have written the words READ THE WORDS and check to make sure they are spelled correctly. Correct any words that are misspelled.

Page 83: Fill in each blank with a word from the Word List. Use each word once. Some sentences have pictures at the end to help you.

Page 84: The following are common words which do not follow the spelling rules. **Use** each sight word once to fill in the blanks.

Page 85: Find the words from Lesson 14 in the WordSearch. Circle the words. The words can be written across, in reverse, or diagonal.

Lesson 15

Page 87: The first twelve words in this list have two syllables. A syllable is a part of a word pronounced as a unit. A syllable consists of a vowel or a vowel with one or more consonants. A syllable has only one vowel sound.

Page 88: Read the sentences. Then put the number of the sentence under the correct picture. **Spelling Dictation** Have someone dictate the words on page 92 to you. After you have written the words READ THE WORDS and check to make sure they are spelled correctly. Correct any words that are misspelled.

Page 89: Fill in each blank with a word from the Word List. Use each word once. Some sentences have pictures at the end to help you.

Page 90: A syllable is a part of a word pronounced as a unit. A syllable consists of a vowel or a vowel with one or more consonants. Each syllable has only one vowel sound. **There** are six types of syllables. One type of syllable is the Closed Syllable. When there are two consonants together with a vowel on each side, the word is divided into syllables between the two consonants. The first syllable is always a closed syllable with a short vowel sound. **Knowing** syllable types and syllable division makes reading and spelling easier. Long words can be broken into syllables and the syllables can be blended together to read or spell the word. **Read** the following words and divide them into syllables. Each word has two closed syllables. The first one has been done for you.

Page 91: Find the words from Lesson 15 in the WordSearch. Circle the words. The words can be written across, in reverse, or diagonal.

Reading and Spelling Check #3

Page 93: Have someone dictate the following words to you, reading down the columns. Write the words. When you have finished writing the words, read the words. At the bottom of this page, write any misspelled words three times. Look up the words in a dictionary if you do not know their meanings.

Lesson 16

Page 94: The first twelve words in this list have two syllables. A syllable is a part of a word pronounced as a unit. A syllable consists of a vowel or a vowel with one or more consonants. A syllable has only one vowel sound.

Page 95: Read the sentences. Then put the number of the sentence under the correct picture. **Spelling Dictation** Have someone dictate the words on page 99 to you. After you have written the words READ THE WORDS and check to make sure they are spelled correctly. Correct any words that are misspelled.

Page 96: Fill in each blank with a word from the Word List. Use each word once. Some sentences have pictures at the end to help you.

Page 97: A syllable is a part of a word pronounced as a unit. A syllable consists of a vowel or a vowel with one or more consonants. Each syllable has only one vowel sound. **There** are six types of syllables. One type of syllable is the Open Syllable. When there is one consonant between two vowels, the word can be divided into syllables before or after the single consonant. The first choice to try is dividing before the consonant. The first syllable will be open and the vowel will be long. When there is a short vowel sound in the first syllable, break after the consonant and the first syllable will be closed. **Knowing** syllable types and syllable division makes reading and spelling easier. Long words can be broken into syllables and the syllables can be blended together to read or spell the word. **Read** the following words and divide them into syllables. Each word has two syllables. Some word's first syllable will be open and others will have a closed first syllable. The first two have been done for you.

Page 98: Find the words from Lesson 16 in the WordSearch. Circle the words. The words can be written across, in reverse, or diagonal.

Lesson 17

Page 100: The first twelve words in this list have two syllables. A syllable is a part of a word pronounced as a unit. A syllable consists of a vowel or a vowel with one or more consonants. A syllable has only one vowel sound.

Page 101: Read the sentences. Then put the number of the sentence under the correct picture. **Spelling Dictation** Have someone dictate the words on page 105 to you. After you have written the words READ THE WORDS and check to make sure they are spelled correctly. Correct any words that are misspelled.

Page 102: Fill in each blank with a word from the Word List. Use each word once. Some sentences have pictures at the end to help you.

Page 103: A syllable is a part of a word pronounced as a unit. A syllable consists of a vowel or a vowel with one or more consonants. Each syllable has only one vowel sound. **Knowing** syllable types and syllable division makes reading and spelling easier. Long words can be broken into syllables and the syllables can be blended together to read or spell the word. **When** there are three consonants between two vowels, the syllable may break before or after the middle consonant. The two consonants that stay together are usually a common blend. **Read** the following words and divide them into syllables. Each word has two syllables. The first one has been done for you.

Page 104: Find the words from Lesson 17 in the WordSearch. Circle the words. The words can be written across, in reverse, or diagonal.

Lesson 18

Page 106: The first twelve words in this list have two syllables. A syllable is a part of a word pronounced as a unit. A syllable consists of a vowel or a vowel with one or more consonants. A syllable has only one vowel sound.

Page 107: Read the sentences. Then put the number of the sentence under the correct picture. **Spelling Dictation** Have someone dictate the words on page 111 to you. After you have written the words READ THE WORDS and check to make sure they are spelled correctly. Correct any words that are misspelled.

Page 108: Fill in each blank with a word from the Word List. Use each word once. Some sentences have pictures at the end to help you.

Page 109: A syllable is a part of a word pronounced as a unit. A syllable consists of a vowel or a vowel with one or more consonants. Each syllable has only one vowel sound. There are six types of syllables. An open syllable has a long vowel sound at the end of the syllable. For example: me, be, my. A closed syllable has a short vowel sound followed by one or more consonants. Example: bug, hill, math. Silent <u>e</u> syllables have silent <u>e</u> at the end of the syllable, which makes the preceding vowel long. Example: dime, sale, bake. These are three types of syllables. **Read** and label the different syllable types. The first one has been done for you.

Page 110: Find the words from Lesson 18 in the WordSearch. Circle the words. The words can be written across, in reverse, or diagonal.

Lesson 19

Page 112: The first twelve words in this list have two syllables. A syllable is a part of a word pronounced as a unit. A syllable consists of a vowel or a vowel with one or more consonants. A syllable has only one vowel sound.

Page 113: Read the sentences. Then put the number of the sentence under the correct picture. **Spelling Dictation** Have someone dictate the words on page 117 to you. After you have written the words READ THE WORDS and check to make sure they are spelled correctly. Correct any words that are misspelled.

Page 114: Fill in each blank with a word from the Word List. Use each word once. Some sentences have pictures at the end to help you.

Page 115: A syllable is a part of a word pronounced as a unit. A syllable consists of a vowel or a vowel with one or more consonants. Each syllable has only one vowel sound. There are six types of syllables. An open syllable has a long vowel sound at the end of the syllable. For example: me, be, my. A closed syllable has a short vowel sound followed by one or more consonants. Examples: bug, hill, math. Silent <u>e</u> syllables have silent <u>e</u> at the end of the syllable, which makes the preceding vowel long. Examples: dime, sale, bake. An <u>r</u> controlled syllable contains a vowel followed by an <u>r</u>. Examples: card, form, her. These are four types of syllables. **Read** the words. Divide each word into syllables. Then label the syllable types. The first one has been done for you.

Page 116: Find the words from Lesson 19 in the WordSearch. Circle the words. The words can be written across, in reverse, or diagonal.

Lesson 20

Page 118: The first twelve words have two syllables. One syllable is a vowel pair syllable. A vowel pair syllable has two vowels together that make one sound. When <u>y</u> and <u>w</u> combine with a vowel to make a vowel sound, <u>y</u> and <u>w</u> are also called vowels.

Page 119: Read the sentences. Then put the number of the sentence under the correct picture. **Spelling Dictation** Have someone dictate the words on page 123 to you. After you have written the words READ THE WORDS and check to make sure they are spelled correctly. Correct any words that are misspelled.

Page 120: Fill in each blank with a word from the Word List. Use each word once. Some sentences have pictures at the end to help you.

134

Page 121: Knowing syllable types and syllable division can make reading and spelling easier. Long words can be broken into syllables and the syllables can be blended together to read or spell the word. There are six types of syllables. The following chart shows five types. **Read** the words. Divide each word into syllables. Then label the syllable types. The first one has been done for you.

Page 122: Find the words from Lesson 20 in the WordSearch. Circle the words. The words can be written across, in reverse, or diagonal.

Reading and Spelling Check #4

Page 124: Have someone dictate the following words to you, reading down the columns. Write the words. When you have finished writing the words, read the words. At the bottom of this page, write any misspelled words three times. Look up the words in a dictionary if you do not know their meanings.

Índice

Index

Books Available From **FISHER HILL**

ENGLISH READING AND SPELLING FOR THE SPANISH SPEAKER Books 1, 2, 3, 4, & 5
For Ages 10-Adult

ENGLISH for the SPANISH SPEAKER Books 1, 2, 3, 4 & Cassettes
For Ages 10 – Adult

SPANISH made FUN and EASY Books 1 & 2
For Ages 10 – Adult

HEALTH Easy to Read
For Ages 10-Adult

United STATES of America Stories, Maps, Activities in Spanish and English Books 1, 2, 3, & 4
For Ages 10 - Adult

English Reading and Spelling for the Spanish Speaker Books 1, 2, 3, 4, & 5 contain twenty lessons to help Spanish-speaking students learn to read and spell English. The books use a systematic approach in teaching the English speech sounds and other phonological skills. They also present basic sight words that are not phonetic. The word lists are in Spanish and English and all directions are in Spanish with English translations. Each book is $14.95 and approximately 142 pages. Book size is 8 1/2 x 11. Book 1 ISBN 1-878253-24-7, Book 2 ISBN 1-878253-25-5, Book 3 ISBN 1-878253-26-3, Book 4 ISBN 1-878253-29-8, Book 5 ISBN 1-878253-30-1.

ENGLISH for the SPANISH SPEAKER Books 1, 2, 3, & 4 are English as a Second Language workbooks for ages 10 - adult. Each book is divided into eight lessons and is written in Spanish and English. Each lesson includes: vocabulary, a conversation, a story, four activity pages, an answer key, two dictionaries: English-Spanish and Spanish-English, a puzzle section, and an index. Each book is $12.95 and approximately 110 pages. Book size is 8 1/2 x 11. Book 1 ISBN 1-878253-07-7, Book 2 ISBN 1-878253-16-6, Book 3 ISBN 1-878253-17-4, Book 4 ISBN 1-878253-18-2; Book 1 Cassette ISBN 1-878253-21-2, Book 2 Cassette ISBN 1-878253-32-8, Book 3 Cassette ISBN 1-878253-33-6, Book 4 Cassette ISBN 1-878253-34-4.

SPANISH made FUN and EASY Books 1 & 2 are workbooks for ages 10 - adult. Each book includes stories, games, conversations, activity pages, vocabulary lists, dictionaries, and an index. The books are for beginning Spanish students; people who want to brush up on high school Spanish; or for Spanish speakers who want to learn how to read and write Spanish. Each book is $14.95 and 134 pages. Book size is 8 1/2 x 11. Book 1 ISBN 1-878253-06-9, Book 2 ISBN 1-878253-19-0.

HEALTH Easy to Read contains 21 easy to read stories. After each story is a vocabulary page, a grammar page, and a question and answer page. The stories are about changing people's life styles to reduce their risk of poor health and premature death. Book is $12.95 and has 118 pages. Book size is 8 1/2 x 11. ISBN 1-878253-22-0; $12.95.

United STATES of America Stories, Maps, Activities in SPANISH and ENGLISH Books 1, 2, 3, & 4 are easy to read books about the United States of America for ages 10 - adult. Each state is presented by a story, map, and activities. Each book contains information for 12 to 13 states and has an answer key and index. The states are presented in alphabetical order. Book size is 8 1/2 x 11. Each book is $14.95 and approximately 140 pages.
Book 1 ISBN 1-878253-23-9 Alabama through Idaho
Book 2 ISBN 1-878253-11-5 Illinois through Missouri
Book 3 ISBN 1-878253-12-3 Montana through Pennsylvania
Book 4 ISBN 1-878253-13-1 Rhode Island through Wyoming

ORDER FORM

Name: _____

Address: _____

_____

Purchase Order Number: _____

Credit Card Number and Expiration Date: _____

We accept Visa and Mastercard only. Please include cardholder's name.

QUANTITY	BOOK TITLE	RETAIL PRICE	AMOUNT
	English Reading and Spelling for the Spanish Speaker Book 1	$14.95	
	English Reading and Spelling for the Spanish Speaker Book 2	$14.95	
	English Reading and Spelling for the Spanish Speaker Book 3	$14.95	
	English Reading and Spelling for the Spanish Speaker Book 4	$14.95	
	English Reading and Spelling for the Spanish Speaker Book 5	$14.95	
	Diccionario Español-Inglés	$5.99	
	English For The Spanish Speaker Book 1	$12.95	
	English For The Spanish Speaker Book 1 Cassette	$10.95	
	English For The Spanish Speaker Book 1 and Cassette	$21.95	
	English For The Spanish Speaker Book 2	$12.95	
	English For The Spanish Speaker Book 2 Cassette	$10.95	
	English For The Spanish Speaker Book 2 and Cassette	$21.95	
	English For The Spanish Speaker Book 3	$12.95	
	English For The Spanish Speaker Book 3 Cassette	$10.95	
	English For The Spanish Speaker Book 3 and Cassette	$21.95	
	English For The Spanish Speaker Book 4	$12.95	
	English For The Spanish Speaker Book 4 Cassette	$10.95	
	English For The Spanish Speaker Book 4 and Cassette	$21.95	
	HEALTH Easy to Read	$12.95	
	USA Stories, Maps, Activities in Spanish & English Book 1	$14.95	
	USA Stories, Maps, Activities in Spanish & English Book 2	$14.95	
	USA Stories, Maps, Activities in Spanish & English Book 3	$14.95	
	USA Stories, Maps, Activities in Spanish & English Book 4	$14.95	
	SPANISH made FUN & EASY Book 1	$14.95	
	SPANISH made FUN & EASY Book 2	$14.95	